REVERSE IN MINISTRY AND MISSIONS: AFRICANS IN THE DARK CONTINENT OF EUROPE

An Historical Study of African Churches in Europe

BY
THE REV ISRAEL OLOFINJANA
B A MTh

authorHOUSE®

AuthorHouse™ UK Ltd.
500 Avebury Boulevard
Central Milton Keynes, MK9 2BE
www.authorhouse.co.uk
Phone: 08001974150

© 2010 Israel Olofinjana. All rights reserved.

No part of this book may be reproduced, stored in a retrieval system, or transmitted by any means without the written permission of the author.

First published by AuthorHouse   5/17/2010

ISBN: 978-1-4490-9549-9 (sc)

This book is printed on acid-free paper.

*Dedicated to African ministers and missionaries
who are labouring tirelessly
to see God's Kingdom grow in Europe*

Endorsements by Church Leaders

"The presence of so many vigorous and committed black churches is one of the bright spots on the horizon of churches in the UK. This work is a pioneering contribution to understanding where these churches are coming from, how they understand their mission in and to the UK and how they are likely to shape the future of Christianity in these islands. It is very welcome."

Dr Nigel Wright, Principal of Spurgeon's College, London

"Rev. Israel has produced a winning combination of research, history and practical theology with this wonderful piece. I believe it is essential reading for every leader who is serious about contemporary cross cultural ministry and mission in 21st century Britain." **Dr Jonathan Oloyede, Convener Global Day of Prayer London**

"It was a privilege to be at the ministers' gathering in Brockley when Israel first presented this work. He shared with us then the fruit of his wide research and we gained much from his insights into the history of African Christianity and the current contribution of African Christians to mission in Europe, 'the dark continent'. I am delighted that his work will now have a wider audience and that more will learn from the scholarship, honesty, perceptiveness and faith that are all reflected in his writing."

John Richardson, Ecumenical Officer, Churches Together in South London

"Rev. Israel Olofinjana highlights the critical issues which Africans are grappling with in their courage to reach Europe. This is a resource for Africans who are doing mission work in contexts beyond the African continent."
Rev. Nicta M. Lubaale, General Secretary, Organisation of African Instituted Churches (OAIC), Nairobi, Kenya

"The title of this excellent book is absolutely right. Europe is, spiritually, a dark continent and it desperately needs people from other lands, and especially Africa, to help us to hear the Good News of Jesus Christ. Israel has written a fascinating account of the way in which missionary movements have changed direction. I thank God for Israel and other Africans like him who are offering a wise and thoughtful ministry amidst all the challenges and cynicism of the European context. I welcome this book and believe that it makes a significant contribution to our understanding of contemporary mission."

Rev. Jonathan Edwards, General Secretary of the Baptist Union of Great Britain

"This work produced by Rev. Israel Olofinjana provides very timely insight into the missional impact of African-led and Black majority Pentecostal churches within the context of 21st century Europe. He summarises the missional history of Africa and analyses how the trend has reversed such that Europe, with Great Britain as a model example, has now become the real mission field while African ministers have courageously risen up to take the mantle of Church missional leadership. This is essential reading for anyone who wants to understand where we are coming from and how to be involved in this current exciting endtime move of God."

Dr Femi Olowo, Principal, South London Christian College

Endorsements by Church Leaders

"This is a fascinating and well researched exploration of the movement of African Christians into Europe within the last decades, and their impact on the church, particularly in Great Britain.

The energy of the writing reflects the energy of the subject, which promises to bring new hope and vitality to a part of the Christian Church that is in alarming decline.

There is much detail here about the presence of Africans in the UK over the centuries, and individuals who have contributed to our life in these islands. The new African churches are documented, with their leaders and their distinctive approaches. The Rev. Olofinjana also offers a critique of the strengths and weaknesses of this movement and raises some interesting questions about how their enthusiasm and commitment might need to develop if the full potential of this movement for re-evangelising Britain is to be realised. For anyone concerned about the decline of the church in the West this study offers an encouraging resume of new flows of life that bring much hope for the future. I warmly commend it."

Rev. Dr. P.M.Took

Acknowledgments

Writing an acknowledgement is not an easy task as you have to decide who to include and who not to. May I say now to those I omitted due to space, please forgive me. Those acknowledged here are people who have contributed in some way to the production of this book. I would especially like to thank my Mother who brought me up with Christian values, especially introducing me to the Pentecostal experience and history, and to my siblings and extended family for their ongoing support.

The substance of this book was firstly written as a research paper presented at Brockley Churches Together in South East London. I want to thank all the local ministers who were present at the discussion for their support and encouragement. Special thanks to John Richardson, ecumenical officer for Churches Together in South London for his enthusiasm about this work. I am grateful to Bishop Dr Joe Aldred of Minority Ethnic Christian Affairs (MECA) for reading through the manuscript of this book and writing a foreword. In addition, I am thankful to Rev. Wale Hudson-Roberts, Racial Justice Co-ordinator for the Baptist Union; Dr Femi Olowo, Principal of South London Christian College; Mr Emmanuel Oladipo, former International Director of Scripture Union; Rev. Joe Kapolyo, minister of Edmonton Baptist Church; Pastor John Palmer, minister at Redeemed Christian Church of God (RCCG) Sanctuary Parish in East London; Rev. Michele Mahon, Youth Specialist at Westbourne Park Baptist Church and Pastor Raphael Amoako-Atta, associate minister at Victory Baptist Church for their willingness to contribute regarding Black

Majority Churches. Special thanks to Dr Jonathan Oloyede for his information and insights that were invaluable to this work. I am also grateful to Rev. Kumar Rajagopalan, Racial Justice minister for London Baptist Association (LBA) for his corrections and advice regarding this work; Rev. Geoffrey Andrews, minister of Perryrise Baptist Church for taking time to read and offer suggestions on the research work; Dr Richard Burgess, research fellow at Birmingham University and Brian Woolnough of Oxford Centre for Mission Studies (OCMS) for their encouragement.

I am indebted to Bill Roberts, who granted me an interview on his experiences as Scripture Union Travelling Secretary in Nigeria and Sierra Leone and for the hospitality shown to me and my wife when we visited. I am also grateful to Dr Kent Hodge and his family for their hospitality, resources and information shared regarding the work of the late Benson Idahosa. I am also thankful to the Cooper family who welcomed me and my wife into their family and Church. I am appreciative of Dr Nigel Wright, Principal of Spurgeon's College; Dr Debra Reid, tutor at Spurgeon's College and Dr Chris Voke, Vice Principal of Spurgeon's College, for their encouragement.

Finally, I am grateful to my colleague, Rev. Carol Bostridge for giving me the time to write this book; without her support this would have been difficult. Lastly, I am grateful to my wife Lucy for painstakingly reading through the manuscript of this book and for her corrections which have made this work what it is today.

Contents

Endorsements by Church Leaders	*vii*
Acknowledgments	*xi*
Foreword	*xv*
Chapter One Introduction	*1*
Purpose of Study	1
Research Methodology	2
Limitations of Research	3
Chapter Two Europeans in the Dark Continent of Africa	*5*
African Christianity and Historical Overview of Christianity in Africa	5
Impact and Contributions of Christian Missions in West Africa	15
Weaknesses and Difficulties of European missions in West Africa	17
Partnership and Renewal: The rise of African Independent Churches, Classic Pentecostals and Interdenominational Evangelical Fellowships in Africa	20
Chapter Three Africans in the Dark Continent of Europe	*28*
Historical Overview of Africans in Europe	28
Contributions of African-led Churches in Diaspora	46
Factors behind the Success of Black Majority Churches (BMCs) Mega Churches in Britain	51
Criticisms of Black Majority Churches (BMCs)	52
Weaknesses of African-led Churches in the UK	56

***Chapter Four Profile of an African Church in Europe: History and Doctrine of Kingsway International Christian Centre (KICC)* 58**
    History and Growth of KICC   **59**
    Beliefs of KICC   **65**
    Practices of KICC   **71**
Chapter Five Concluding Observations   *73*
Glossary   *75*
Bibliography   *78*
About the Author   83

Foreword

Reverse in ministry and missions offers an exciting insight in an area of research that is virtually unexplored. I was aware that European missionaries had taken their culturally embellished denominationalised version of Christianity to Africa as elsewhere in the colonial world. I was also aware that many Africans, like Caribbean people before them, had travelled to Britain during the second half of the 20th Century and some had set up churches. However having both of these developments explored through the prism of mission and ministry from an African point of view is refreshing indeed. I believe it is an old African proverb that says, until the lions have their own historians, tales of the hunt will always glorify the hunter. It is important to hear tales of the hunt from both sides and we have volumes about the tales of African/European mission, but alas, little from the African perspective. This work redresses the balance a little, but there is much more to do.

Opinions are divided concerning the role of European missionaries in Africa. Were they a force for good or ill? A balanced view might lead us to the conclusion that they did both. It will be difficult to convince some that European Christianity did not simply conspire to undermine authentic African religious institutions and beliefs, and simultaneously customise and condition the African mind to look up to whiteness as superior to blackness. African luminaries like Edward Wilmot Blyden believe that Islam did more for African self-development and self-esteem than Christianity ever did. But I happen to know many Africans who hold firmly to the view that European missionaries did more good for Africa than bad. Here, the author of this work is at pains to point out that Christianity, without its European garb, was in Africa long before the European slave traders with missionaries in tow arrived.

John Mbiti's truism that Africans are incurably religious is given further credence when we note the rise of African-led churches and movements in Britain. People who may have come as education and economic migrants are the inspiration behind some of the largest and fastest growing churches in Britain's history. They exert unquestionable impact on British society. But the author of this work is correct to point out that these churches need to rise to even higher and newer dimensions if their ministry is to extend beyond the circumstantially imposed national, ethnic and cultural boundaries within which they continue to exist. Nothing less than a mission to the wider communities among whom they live will do and in this regard the continuing presence of specifically Black or African churches undercut the notion that Africans have come to do mission and ministry in reverse.

European missionaries succeeded in taking their understanding of the Gospel of Jesus to the Africans in Africa. The challenge of the 21st Century is, can Africans become successful in taking the Gospel of Jesus to Europeans in Europe who have become hardened and indeed darkened to the Gospel of Jesus? The jury is still out and it will be interesting to watch what this cross-cultural mission looks like in the years to come. Reverse in Ministry and Missions has certainly started a worthwhile conversation.

Bishop Dr Joe Aldred,

Churches Together in England.

Chapter One
Introduction

Purpose of Study

John Pobee, an African theologian, said in his foreword to the book 'African Reformation', "It is a contemporary mantra of the study of Church History and Missiology that the centre of gravity of world Christianity has shifted from the North Atlantic to the South, with Africa, Asia, Latin America and the Pacific as the new heartland of Christianity".[1] Pobee observed this in recognition of the fact that Christianity is growing by leaps and bounds in the Two-Thirds World, whereas it is on the decline in the West.

Africa is part of the Two-Thirds World where the expression of Christianity that is growing is Pentecostalism. Two stages have been identified in the history of African Pentecostalism, the first has been labelled African Instituted Churches (AICs) and the second Neo-Pentecostal Churches (NPCs) or Charismatic Churches. Apart from revival, another reason for the explosion in growth in these Churches has been because Africans are taking the initiative, leading fellow Africans and successfully adapting Christianity to African culture and context. This increase in Church growth in Africa eventually led to another shift which has been recognised by anthropologists, missiologists and religious scholars. This has been the efforts of Africans in reaching out to the Western World. African ministers and missionaries are on the increase,

---
1   Allan H. Anderson, *African Reformation*, Eritrea, African World Press, Forward, 2001.

crossing over to Europe to share the Gospel. There are many factors explaining this recent shift, but one of significance is the conviction of the majority of African ministers and missionaries that Europe has become too secular and forgotten its Christian roots; in essence the decline of Christianity in Europe has been attributed to its coldness towards religion, especially Christianity.

The purpose of this book is to shed more light on the significant contributions of African ministers and missionaries in Europe. In order to do this, there is the need to first consider the missionary efforts of Europeans to Africans in the nineteenth century. Therefore I shall begin with an historical overview of European missions to the 'dark continent of Africa'. I shall be looking at the positive impact of their missionary enterprises as well as weaknesses of their mission. Understanding the positive contributions of European missionaries in Africa is vital for the reverse missions by African ministers and missionaries in Europe. As Rev. Kingsley Appaigyei, President of the Baptist Union 2009-2010 observed, those of us who are African Christians ministering in the UK now are directly or indirectly a harvest of the seeds sown by the early missionaries to Africa.[2] In the third chapter, I shall attempt a second historical overview, this time of African missionary efforts in the 'dark continent of Europe'. In addition, I will look at the significant contributions of African-led Churches in Britain and some of their impact on global Christianity, as well as areas where they are failing in their mission to Europeans. Attention is given to the factors behind the success of black Churches in the UK, as well as criticisms levied against them. The fourth chapter considers the history and doctrine of an African Neo-Pentecostal Church in Britain, KICC, as a case study to illustrate the development and growth of African Churches in Europe.

---

2   *The Baptist Times*, Thursday 6th of August, 2009

Research Methodology

One of my research methods has been that of a participant observer, as I am an African minister living and ministering in the UK. This has afforded me the opportunity to meet other African ministers and missionaries serving here. In my field research I have attended seminars, conferences, Church services and festivals that are relevant to this subject. In addition to this insiders' perspective, I have also interviewed eight African ministers and missionaries living in the UK. These ministers are drawn from different Church traditions and nationalities. Four of them are Baptist ministers, three Pentecostals and one works in an interdenominational capacity. Six are Nigerians, while the remaining two are a Zambian and a Ghanaian. One is a woman. I would have preferred to have interviewed more women, but the truth is that there are few women who are African ministers. This interview has been in the form of questionnaires emailed to these ministers, the reason for this approach being the busy schedules of these ministers. I have also interviewed two British missionaries who are still serving in Africa. One had ministered in Nigeria and is now ministering in Sierra Leone. The other is serving in Nigeria. Finally, I have consulted and used both primary and secondary materials in carrying out this research. These have been in the form of books, magazines, Church websites and welcome booklets of some of the Churches or Ministries mentioned.

Limitations of Research

The title of this book reads 'Reverse in Ministry and Missions: Africans in the Dark Continent of Europe'. I must caution here that I am not attempting to document the efforts of all the African ministers in Europe; rather I shall be looking at my immediate context, Britain, as a case study for Europe. As Britain is my ministerial niche, I shall make only few references to the work of African ministers in other parts of Europe. In addition to this, when considering the history and contributions of the Black Majority Churches (BMC) in Britain, I have limited this to two strands; the Caribbean Christians and the African Christians. I have not considered the efforts of South American Christians in Britain, such as the Brazilian Churches. The reason has been my inadequate knowledge of these Churches. For the purpose of this research I have narrowed my discussions to the role of Africans, whilst making references to the Caribbean contributions.

Another caution I need to sound is that in doing an historical overview of European missionaries in Africa, I have limited this to West Africa. References will be made to other parts of Africa, but West Africa, where I originate, is my concern in this book. Finally, it must be borne in mind that seven out of my eight respondents are men; therefore this work is limited in terms of African women ministries. I do hope that this work will inspire others to research into African women who are involved in ministry.

Chapter Two
Europeans in the Dark Continent of Africa

African Christianity and Historical Overview of Christianity in Africa

There is the general assumption today that Christianity first came to Africa through the missionary efforts of the Europeans in the nineteenth century. This is an incorrect assumption as Christianity was in Africa as early as the first century AD. However, before unpacking this, attention is drawn to some antecedents in Scripture about our Lord's contact with Africa. According to Matthew's Gospel, baby Jesus was taken to Egypt in North Africa for safety when Herod the Great was killing all baby boys who were two years old (Matthew 2: 13-18). The second contact of our Lord with Africa was towards the end of his life. Mark, which has been accorded the oldest Gospel in the New Testament, recorded that one Simon of Cyrene (a Roman Province in Libya, North Africa, which had a large Jewish population), father of Alexander and Rufus, was compelled by the Roman soldiers to help Jesus carry His cross on His way to Golgotha (Mark 15: 21). The third encounter was between Africa and the Church on the day of Pentecost when the Church was commissioned (Acts 2: 1-13). Among the pilgrims who had come to the Jewish Feast of Pentecost and witnessed the outpouring of the Holy Spirit on the disciples were people from Egypt and Cyrene (part of Libya). This becomes significant if it is understood that Pentecost was the birth of the Church. These three incidents appear somewhat prophetic considering the fact that Christianity later flourished in North Africa in the second and third century AD.

The next phase in Church history, according to Luke the historian, was the scattering of the new believers as a result of the martyrdom of Stephen (Acts 7: 54-8: 1-3). The believers were scattered all over Judea and Samaria. Among those who were scattered were Cyrenians (North Africans) who spread the Gospel to places such as Antioch in Syria. It was in Antioch that the believers were first called Christians (Acts 11: 19-26). Acts 13 which details the call of Saul and Barnabas mentions Lucius of Cyrene and 'Simeon called Niger' (meaning Black). The involvement of North Africans in the establishment of the Church in Antioch obviously demonstrates that Africans were active participants in mission from the beginning of the Church.

The episode of Christianity in Africa most well known is the story of the Ethiopian Eunuch's encounter with Philip (Acts 8: 26-40). Ethiopia in this period has been identified by scholars as Upper Egypt and Sudan, between Aswan and Khartoum. Being an important official in the Queen's court, it is probable that this man spread the Gospel in Nubia in North Africa. Eusebius the Church historian mentioned in his Ecclesiastical History that this man preached the Gospel to his native country men, see Eusebius 2: 1.[3] A further attempt to understand how Christianity came to Africa has been the long tradition that Mark, identified as the spiritual son of Apostle Peter and traditionally accepted as the author of Mark's Gospel, went and preached the Gospel in Egypt. On this Eusebius has this to say:

> *Mark is said to have been the first man to set out for Egypt and preach there the Gospel which he had himself written down, and the first to establish Churches in Alexandria itself* (Eusebius 2: 16).[4]

---
3   Eusebius, *The History of the Church*, Middlesex, England, Penguin Books, 1965, pp 37-38.
4   Eusebius., p. 50.

Whether this tradition is valid or not, it is clear that Christianity was well established in Alexandria and Carthage in North Africa towards the end of the second century. In fact these places were seen as Christian centres alongside Jerusalem, Antioch and Rome. The Churches in North Africa were characterised by martyrs, theologians, monks and renowned catechetical Schools of higher learning. For example Apollos, one of the eminent figures in the New Testament, was a native of Alexandria in Egypt (Acts 18: 18-28). Regarding martyrs, it must be recalled that it was in one of the amphi-theatres in Carthage that the famous martyrdoms of Perpetua and Felicita occurred c. AD 203.[5] The persecution which the Churches in North Africa faced made them stronger and caused them to increase. Tertullian (c. AD 150- 225) said concerning one of the sons of the soil *'the blood of the martyrs is the seed of the Church'* (Tertullian, Apology, book 50).[6]

North Africa has produced the greatest theologians of the Patristic era (c. AD 100-700). These included men such as Clement of Alexandria (c. AD 150-215) who presided over the Catechetical School in Alexandria, Egypt (this Catechetical School has been regarded as the first Theological Institution in history). Clement was one of the earliest Christians to use Greek philosophy to interpret Christian teachings. Another figure who has been identified as one of the Fathers of the Eastern Church is Origen (c. AD 185-253). He succeeded Clement as the Head of the Catechetical School, but also in addition he laid the foundations for the science of textual criticism and Biblical hermeneutics. Another African Church father is Tertullian (c. AD 150-225) who contributed immensely to Western Christianity and theology and has been regarded as the Father of Latin Christianity. Tertullian was from Carthage, present day Morocco, Tunisia and Algeria. Tertullian is remembered as coining the word 'Trinity' and was a fierce apologetic that defended the Gospel against

---

5   Perpetua was a 22 year old widow. She was killed alongside her slave girl, Felicita, who was expecting a child. They died hand in hand refusing to deny Christ.
6   http://www.ccel.org/ccel/schaff/anf03.iv.iii.l.html.

heretics. Other giants of the faith from North Africa whose influence resounds today in Eastern Orthodoxy and Western theology are Cyprian, Bishop of Carthage (c. AD 200-258); Athanasius of Alexandria (c. AD 293-373) and Augustine of Hippo (c. AD 354-431). Apart from Apostle Paul, Augustine has been regarded as one of the greatest thinkers of all time. However many do not realise that Augustine was also from North Africa, specifically Thagaste (modern Algeria).

The history above reveals that Christianity in its early stages was very strong in Africa and Africa should been seen in connection with the development of mainstream Christianity both in the East and in the West. However, Christianity later died out in these regions, with the exception of Ethiopia and some parts of Egypt which indigenised Christianity among the Copts.[7] The reason for the decline of Christianity in North Africa was a combination of several factors: the unhealthy view about martyrdom, schisms in the Church (the Donatist controversy), the strict rigorist attitude of some Church members, the lack of indigenisation of Roman Latin Christianity among the Berbers of North Africa and the religious politics between Constantinople (Byzantine) and Egypt as played out in the different Church Councils. Therefore when Islam arrived in the seventh century it met a divisive and weak Christianity. The Berbers in North Africa consequently accepted Islam against the religion of their Roman oppressors, Christianity. This complete the first stage of Christianity in Africa

The first stage of planting Christianity in Africa goes back to the Middle Ages, starting with the attempts of Roman Catholic Orders to propagate the faith in North Africa and the Catholic Portuguese explorers in fifteenth century West Africa. Muslim occupation of some parts of Africa prohibited any form of Christian proselytising. This considerably hindered the spread of the Gospel, but despite this restriction two Roman Catholic

---

7   The Ethiopian Orthodox Church and the Coptic Church survived respectively in Ethiopia and Egypt.

Orders, the Franciscans and the Dominicans, undertook to spread the Gospel in Muslim occupied territories in Africa. It is recorded that Francis of Assisi (the pioneer of the Franciscan Order) risked his life by preaching the Gospel before the Muslim Sultan during the fourth crusade. This act of boldness was emulated by his monks who later suffered martyrdom. The Dominicans on the other hand had a different approach to missions in Africa. They worked amongst Christian soldiers and slaves and were therefore able to engage with Muslims, especially those on the brink of apostasy. The Dominicans, as preaching Friars, believed in educating monks in how to engage non-Christians with the Gospel message; in this case Muslims. As a result of their preaching vocation they sought to present the Gospel in a reasonable way. It was for this reason that Raymond Penafort, a Dominican Friar, approached the great medieval scholastic St Thomas Aquinas. This is recorded in Aquinas theological work, '*Summa contra Gentiles*'; 'Summary against the Gentiles'.

Africa south of the Sahara met Christianity in the fifteenth century through the Portuguese explorers. The Portuguese had being trading in gold, ivory and slaves with West Africa through the Moors of North Africa; this was known as the Trans-Saharan trade. However the Portuguese wanted to remove the middlemen and trade directly with West Africa. In addition they desired to trade with India on the East side of Africa in order to compete with the Venetians who had long being trading with the people of Asia. These commercial reasons led to the explorations of the coast of West Africa. As these lands were being 'discovered' the Portuguese explorers felt the need to propagate the Gospel; they reasoned that in order to over throw the Muslims in the North they needed Christian kings as allies to assist them. They also felt that the people of West Africa, already perceived as pagans, needed to hear the Gospel.

A Papal bull was granted by the Pope (Alexander VI) conferring the responsibility of missions in the newly found lands to the King of Portugal. This bull or treaty also excluded all other Europeans from trading in West Africa. Explorers such as Prince Henry the Navigator (1394-1460) acquired and developed huge maps, charts, globes and several instruments for navigation. He was a pioneer and laid the foundations for other explorers to build on. Men such as Vasco da Gama (1460-1524) and Bartholomew Diaz followed in his footsteps. It was Bartholomew who discovered Cabo Tormentoso in 1486 (The Cape of Storm), which was later renamed Cabo de Bona Esperanca (The Cape of Good Hope, in what is now South Africa). Gil Eannes discovered Cape Bojador in 1434 (now Morocco).

Other coasts that were discovered include:

- Sierra Leone
- Cabo Mesurado (now modern Monrovia in Liberia)
- Rio de Oro (now between Morocco and Mauritania), discovered in 1435
- Cape Verde (opposite Mauritania and Senegal)
- Gambia
- El Mina (Modern Ghana)
- Lagos in Nigeria (Lagos was the name of a seaport in Portugal)
- Bights of Benin and Biafra (South-Eastern Nigeria)
- Guinea coast (which includes Ivory Coast and Cameroon)
- Congo.

The Portuguese soon established a profitable trade with the people of Africa. The commodities in which they traded were gold, slaves, ivory, pepper, gum and ostrich feathers. These were exchanged for cheap cloth, beads, trinkets, cowry shells and some hardware such as cooking pots, brass pans and iron rods. The trade in slaves later developed into the Trans-

Chapter Two Europeans in the Dark Continent of Africa

Atlantic slave trade. One major reason for this was that in 1492 Spain brought to the attention of the peoples of Europe that there were lands rich for cultivation and natives living in the West Indies and America. Man power was needed to work the sugar and tobacco plantations as well as the gold and silver mines in the new lands. Slaves in Africa became the victims and source of manpower that was needed to work in America and the West Indies. Portugal held the monopoly of this trade in the fifteenth and most of the sixteenth century. It must be mentioned that in 1580 Portugal became part of the Spanish empire under King Philip II and remained as such until around 1640. This means that Spain then occupied and dominated all the territory owned by Portugal in Africa. The majority of the European countries such as England, France, Holland, Denmark and Sweden were enemies of the Spanish empire and therefore they were in competition with Spain both in the New Worlds and in Africa. This eventually led to the involvement of the other European nations mentioned above in the Trans-Atlantic slave trade.

In their attempt to spread Christianity the Portuguese explorers first converted the African chiefs and kings. They reasoned that these men had authority over their subjects; therefore they could command their subjects to obey the faith. The Chief of Gambia was converted in 1456 and in 1485 Behenoi the Chief of Wolf (Senegambia) sought alliance with the Portuguese. The condition for the alliance was for Behenoi to be converted to Christianity. Other African chiefs and kings who were converted include the King of Warri (Southern Nigeria), the King of Benin and King Fetu of the Gold Coast (Ghana). The spread of Christianity in West Africa was successful in some parts of the continent, but on the whole this second attempt at planting Christianity in Africa was not sustained. There are several factors that caused the failure of the Portuguese missions. The crusader spirit of spreading Christianity in Africa was one notable factor; this was particularly so with the *requerimiento* ideology of the Spanish monarchs which asserted that God and the papal successors had sovereign rights over the earth. The Papal bull conferred the title of American and African natives to the Portuguese, therefore rejection of the Gospel could attract hostility. The commercial trade being hand-in-hand with Christianity also did not help genuine conversion. For example, the reason the *oba* (King) of Benin accepted Christianity was because of military support and ammunitions from the Portuguese rather than genuine conversion to the Christian faith. In addition, given that one of the main aims of Portuguese explorers was trade and the capacity to expand trading, there was more interest given to business than spreading the Gospel. Another factor was the assumption that once the chiefs and the kings were converted the natives would automatically follow. This did not allow for genuine and lasting conversion because the subjects were force to accept Christianity rather than choose. Other reasons for the failure of the mission were the hostile climate, shortage of priests and the domination which the slave trade eventually had on the relationship between Europeans and Africans.

The second attempt at spreading Christianity in Africa occurred during the nineteenth century. Several factors are responsible for this third attempt at planting Christianity in Africa:

1. The drive for missions into unknown territories as a result of the Evangelical Revival (in England) and the Great Awakening (in America) in the middle of the eighteenth century.

2. The abolition of the slave trade in 1807 and the need to totally eradicate slavery in the hinterland of Africa.

3. The foundation of the Crown Colonies of Freetown in Sierra (1787) and Liberia (1821) by England and America respectively. Slaves were returned to these colonies from both England and America, and later these slaves began to emigrate to different parts of Africa. These were the people who saw the need for Christianity to be planted in their homelands.

- The Baptist Church: Southern Baptist Convention of United States 1850.
- The Roman Catholic Church: Society for African Missions (SMA) 1868, and later the Society of Holy Ghost Fathers, the White Fathers and Sisters and Lyon Missions.
- Northern Ireland Presbyterian Church: Qua Ibo Church 1877.
- The Sudan Interior Missions (SIM) 1893. They later partnered with African Evangelicals and formed Evangelical Church of West Africa in 1954 (ECWA).
- Dutch Reformed Church of South Africa (Netherlands) 1913.

Apart from the fact that the Mission Churches were from different denominations, they were also from different countries. Some have already been mentioned above, such as Ireland, Scotland, America and the Netherlands, the remaining countries are as follows:

- Germany: The Berlin Missionary Society and the Bremen Mission 1847.
- Switzerland: The Basel Evangelical Society 1827.
- Norway: The Nordic Mission.

There was cooperation among the missionary societies, for example the vice president of CMS once presided over the annual gathering of the Wesleyan Methodist Society. In 1810 William Carey of the BMS, a true pioneer of missions, called for a union of all the societies to meet at the Cape of Good Hope in South Africa.[8] This ecumenical vision was not realised until a hundred years later in Edinburgh, Scotland. This year is the centenary celebration of that gathering which will take place in Edinburgh.

It was in this age of missionary effort that men and women

---

8   G. A. Oshitelu, *Expansion of Christianity in West Africa*, Abeokuta, Nigeria, Visual Resources Publishers, 2002, p. 35.

such as Hannah Kilham, a Quaker missionary in Sierra and Gambia (1774-1832); Robert Moffat, missionary Africa (1795-1883); Henry Venn, CMS missionary and pioneer of indigenous missions in West Africa (1796-1873); Thomas Birth Freeman, a Methodist missionary who operated in West Africa (1809-1890); Hope Waddell, the Presbyterian missionary who laboured in Calabar, Eastern Nigeria (1804-1895); Henry Townsend, a CMS missionary in West Africa (1815-1886); David Livingstone, a missionary to South Africa (1813-1873); Mary Slessor, a Scottish missionary in Calabar, Nigeria (1848-1915); Father Joseph Shanahan, a Catholic missionary who served in Eastern Nigeria (1871-1931) and many others all ministered tirelessly to fulfil the Great Commission. This missionary age also produced education, hospitals and social infrastructures for the Africans. The missions in West Africa were successful to the extent that they produced local clergies such as Bishop Samuel Ajayi Crowther of Nigeria (the first African Bishop), his son, Archdeacon Dandeson Coates Crowther and Rev James Johnson from Sierra Leone who later became Bishop of Niger-Delta Pastorate in Nigeria. These men later pioneered and inspired a new generation of Africans in leading nationalist movements calling for the emancipation of Africans from their colonial masters. These nationalist movements eventually led to the independence of African states in the 1950s and 60s. The second attempt or third as some would argue at planting Christianity was more successful than those previously, although it must be mentioned that the mission had its weaknesses. Before discussing the weaknesses, it is reasonable to highlight the positive contributions of the missionaries to Africa.

Impact and Contributions of Christian Missions in West Africa

❖ Through the contact of Europeans with West Africa coastal states and seaports developed. These included coastal cities such as Elmina (Ghana), Accra (Ghana), Bonny (Nigeria), Lagos (Nigeria), Calabar (Nigeria), Opobo (Nigera) and Freetown (Sierra Leone).

- European trade created more trading opportunities for the people of West Africa.

- The Portuguese explorers introduced many varieties of crop into West Africa. Most of these crops were from America and West Indies. These included sugar cane, maize, pineapple, pawpaw, guava, sweet potato, tobacco and cassava. Oranges, melons, lemons and some other fruits came from Portugal itself.

- The greatest achievement of the European missions was in the area of education. The missionaries regarded education as an indispensable tool in evangelism. It was to this effect that Fourah Bay College was created in Sierra Leone to train African clergies in 1828. The creation of Schools, Colleges and Universities would later be used by the African elite in the emancipation of Africa.

- Bible translation and linguistic study enhanced Africans' ability to read the Bible in their native languages as well transforming their languages into writing. For example, Hannah Kilham (through her linguistic skills) in 1827 produced the first written words of West African Languages. Bishop Samuel Ajayi Crowther also translated the English Bible into Yoruba; in addition, he also reduced the Yoruba language into written form.

- In their effort to reach out to Africans the missionaries establish the printing press. This form of media was later used by the African Nationalist movement in their campaign for the independence of African states.

- The missionary impact of the Europeans can also be seen in the development of health services for Africans. Hospitals, maternity homes, dispensaries and clinics were built by the mission Churches. In addition, the missionaries fought against diseases through vaccination. The introduction of quinine in 1854 to treat malaria was a breakthrough in Africa.

- ❖ The Christian missions played an active role in ending slavery in Africa
- ❖ Politically the missionaries were able, to some extent, to bring together under one rule tribes that were normally at war with each other and in collaboration with the colonial government brought political stability to the people of Africa

Weaknesses and Difficulties of European missions in West Africa

- ❖ The combination of colonisation hand-in-hand with Christian missions led to the idea that 'pagan dark Africa' had to be 'saved by Christian civilised Europe'.
- ❖ The demeaning effects of the slave trade coloured the relationship between the Europeans and Africans.
- ❖ The race theory of the German anthropologist Johann Friedrich Blumenbach (1752-1840), in which the Caucasian race (White) was viewed as far superior to the Negroid race (Black), was used to establish the racial dominance of Europeans over Africans. This combined with the Hamitic theology of the Church finally established the model that Africans were always inferior to Europeans.[9] This Eurocentric attitude led to the total condemnation and misunderstanding of African religions, culture and customs, hence European control over their mission Churches in West Africa.
- ❖ Eurocentrism has been ingrained into the African

---

9 Hamitic theology was developed from the story of when Noah became drunk (Genesis 9: 20-27). When he later realised that his youngest son Ham saw him in his nakedness, Noah cursed Ham's son Canaan pronouncing him a slave to his brothers. Cush, one of Ham's descendants, has been categorised as black as a result of identifying him with Ethiopia, Nubia and Egypt (Genesis 10: 6-14). Therefore some have interpreted the curse on Ham as a curse on black skin colour (Negroid). This theology has been used to justify slavery and oppression of Africans and Native Americans as well as the colonisation of these lands. The problem however is that this has been based on false hermeneutics. Canaan was the person cursed not Cush. Therefore the Biblical story functions to legitimate the conquest of Canaan and the destruction of its inhabitants by the Israelites.

yche and the result has been that Africans have veloped an inferiority complex. This is why to this y Africans blindly follow Western Culture.

- In their passion to convert Africans from their Traditional Religions and culture the missionaries condemned everything African, including African music, art, architecture, dancing and marriage customs. African names were even rejected for baptism, for example Mojola Agbebi in his campaign for cultural nationalism changed his name from David Brown Vincent. Parental authority, which is very dear to African culture, was also undermined.

- The trade that was established between Europe and Africa plundered and exploited African resources. A good example is the African art works in the African section of the British Museum.

- The mission Churches failed to secure the establishment of African clergy to lead their fellow Africans. A good example was the case of Bishop Crowther whose missionary efforts in the Niger expedition of 1841 were later pronounced a failure by the Europeans. Crowther was forced to resign in favour of a European Bishop. This did not encourage the establishment of local clergies and this eventually led to the African Church movement which broke away from the historic Churches in the latter part of the nineteenth century.

- The 'scramble for Africa' which led to partitioning and colonisation towards the end of the nineteenth century treated Africans as commodities and fragmented African identity. This is why there are Anglophone, Francophone and Lusophone African countries. The Berlin conference of 1884/85 laid the foundation of Western imperialism as European nations adopted the principle of 'divide and rule'. In addition it was at this conference that Africa was pronounced as a 'dark continent' because the hinterland remained mysterious and unknown to European explorers.

- The partitioning of Africa among European nations has caused permanent identity crises which have had resounding effects on modern Africa. When the partitioning was being undertaken imperial powers ignored ethnic groupings. The result was that peoples of the same ancestry were divided into two or more states under different European overlords. For example, the Yorubas were divided between French Dahomey (Republic of Benin) and British Nigeria and the Ewes were split between German Togoland and British Gold Coast (now Ghana). Some of the civil and tribal wars in modern Africa have their roots in this partitioning.

- The mission Churches also failed because they encountered other difficulties, for example malaria played a key factor in causing the deaths of the missionaries. This is why Africa was termed 'the White man's grave'.

- A further setback was the vastness of the continent compared with the inadequate number of missionaries and resources available.

- The lack of transport and communication systems faced by the Europeans also hindered missionary efforts. Europeans had to travel long roads in bush pathways on foot or bicycles.

- The language barrier was another difficulty which Europeans had to overcome.

- As a result of the slave trade all white missionaries became suspected as slave masters. This affected the relationship between missionaries and the natives.

Partnership and Renewal: The rise of African Independent Churches, Classic Pentecostals and Interdenominational Evangelical Fellowships in Africa

Having surveyed the contributions and failures of European missions in Africa in the nineteenth century, there is the need to consider European missions in Africa in the twentieth century. This consideration begins with the African Churches or Ethiopian Churches as they were called in Southern Africa.[10] The African Church Movement began due to several factors. Firstly, the refusal and ill-treatment of African clergies by European missions led to secession. The pronouncement of the failure of Bishop Ajayi Crowther of Nigeria and his humiliation by two younger English clergies demonstrated to Africans that indigenous leadership was rejected. Secondly, the translation of the Bible into African languages from around 1840 meant that Africans could now read the Bible. Many of them saw a contradiction in the European mission's attitude and what the New Testament portrays about Christian character. Thirdly, nationalistic spirit was building up among the African elites who had been exposed to Western forms of education. The majority of these elites were also Churchmen. Finally, the lack of understanding and utter condemnation of African culture and customs by some Europeans made matters worse. These factors led to African Churches separating from the Mission Churches. Despite the secession of these Churches from their parent Churches, their organisational structures, styles of leadership, doctrinal positions, rites and rituals remained identical with the Mission Churches. The secession happened in West Africa, particularly in Ghana and Nigeria, in East

---

10 Ethiopianism is the term used to express African nationalism as Ethiopia, apart from Egypt, was the first kingdom to express and revolt against imperialism and white supremacy. The African Church Movement or Ethiopian Churches were a movement formed by the combination of African clergies and laity revolting against white leadership and white control of missions among Africans. In addition, the African Church Movement led African nationalism that resulted in the independence of many African States.

Africa, especially in Kenya and Uganda, and in South Africa. The African Churches separated from Anglican, Methodist, Presbyterian, Baptists and Congregational Churches. For example, the following Churches seceded from the Mission Churches in Nigeria:

- ➢ The Native Baptist Church separated from the Lagos Baptist Church, which belonged to the American Southern Baptists, in 1888.
- ➢ The United Native African Church (UNA) was formed by members of Anglican and Methodists Churches in 1891.
- ➢ The Bethel African Church seceded from C.M.S St Paul's Church, Breadfruit, Lagos in 1901.
- ➢ The United African Methodist Church, Eleja, Lagos also seceded from the Methodist Church in 1917.

The nationalistic concern of these African Churches and the lack of support from the Mission Churches soon jeopardised the evangelistic thrust of the former. This ushered in another era in the Christian history of Africa, the era of African Independent Churches, although their history in some parts of Africa overlaps with that of African Churches.

African Independent Churches, as the name implies, were Churches started by Africans for Africans and were independent financially and organisationally from Mission Churches. African Independent Churches (AICs hereafter) are also called African Instituted Churches, African Indigenous Churches or African Initiated Churches. They were Churches founded by Africans in reaction to the largely lethargic Christianity introduced by the Mission Churches in Africa. Many of these Churches began as prayer groups and later metamorphosed into Church denominations, and revival played a dominant role in the Churches' birth and growth. These Churches have different names in different parts of Africa, for example in Ghana they are known as *Sumsum sore* (Spirit Churches), in Nigeria they are best known as *Aladura* Churches *(Aladura* meaning 'the praying people'), in East Africa they are termed *Roho* Churches (Churches of the Spirit) and *Arathi* (Prophets) and in South Africa they are called Zion or Apostolic Churches. Some characteristics of these Churches are prophetism, healing, spirit possession, zionistic tendencies, loud prayers, Old Testament emphasis and charismatic leadership. Many of these Churches indigenised Christianity among their own people and this is one of the reasons why they experienced tremendous revival and growth. For example, polygamy was a respected marriage institution in the majority of African states. This was condemned by the Europeans to the extent that when someone with two wives became a Christian and wanted to be baptised, he was asked to leave one of his wives before he could be accepted for baptism. The practice of polygamy was accommodated by some AICs which accepted people with two wives into their assembly.

The following lists a number of the AICs:

- The Harrist Churches in West Africa, founded by the followers of the Liberian Prophet William Wade Harris after his death (1865-1929).
- Christ Army Church in Nigeria, founded by the followers of Garrick Sokari Braide also after his death of (1882-1918).
- Musama Disco Christo Church (Army of the Cross of Christ), founded in 1924 by Prophet Jemisemiham Jehu-Appiah (1893-1948) and Abena Bawa, later named Hannah Barnes.
- The Kimbanguist Church in Central Africa, founded by Prophet Simon Kimbangu (1887-1951).
- Zion Christian Church was founded in South Africa in 1925 by Engenas Lekganyane (1880-1948).
- Eternal Sacred Order of Cherubim and Seraphim (C&S) started in 1925 by Prophet Moses Orimolade Tunolase (1879-1933) in Nigeria.

- Christ Apostolic Church (CAC), founded in Nigeria in 1941. This Church is usually attributed as founded by Joseph Ayodele Babalola (1904-1959) who led a massive revival in the 1930s. This Church had its origins in a prayer group that started around 1918.
- The Church of the Lord Aladura (CLA) was founded by Josiah Ositelu (1902-1966) in Nigeria around 1930.
- Celestial Church of Christ (CCC) was founded in 1947 by S. B. J Oschoffa (1909-1985) in Port Novo, Republic of Benin but this Church flourished more in Nigeria.

Around the same period that AICs were formed and expanding in Africa, Classic Pentecostal Churches from both North America and Britain were sending missionaries to Africa. One reason for this was the Azusa Street revival of 1906 which gave birth to movements such as Apostolic Faith Mission, Assemblies of God and Foursquare Gospel Church. Apostolic Faith Mission operated more in South Africa through the efforts of John G. Lake, whilst Assemblies of God and Foursquare Gospel Church operated more in West and East Africa in the twentieth century. The British Apostolic, founded by W. J. Williams and his brother D. P. Williams, were influenced by the Welsh revival of 1904 and sent missionaries to West Africa. The Apostolic missionaries partnered with African Instituted Churches such as the Faith Tabernacle members of Nigeria and Ghana (Faith Tabernacle later became Christ Apostolic Church both in Ghana and Nigeria). It was West African Christians who actually invited missionaries from The Apostolic Church in Britain and Assemblies of God in North America to come to West Africa. In response to this request Idris Vaughan and George Perfect were sent by the Apostolic Church of Britain in 1932 to Nigeria, and James Mckeown to Ghana in 1937. Assemblies of God sent Rev. W. L. Shirer and his wife to consolidate the revival which had already broken out in South-eastern Nigeria in 1939. This led to the start of Assemblies of God in Nigeria. This collaboration between Westerners and Africans demonstrated a new missionary attitude viewing African Christians as equal partners rather than as inferior 'savages', the predominant thinking amongst the earlier missionaries. Although there were schisms in the Church with Christ Apostolic Church (CAC) seceding from the UK Apostolic Church both in Nigeria and Ghana respectively, it must however be mentioned that other Africans remained faithful to the UK Apostolic Church. The UK Apostolic Church today is known as The Apostolic Church in Nigeria (TAC) and the Church of Pentecost in Ghana.[11]

The partnership that existed between Classic Pentecostal missionaries and African Instituted members led to revival in certain quarters. For example, Idris Vaughan of the UK Apostolic Church led a revival in Calabar, South-eastern Nigeria in 1933.[12] Another UK Apostolic Church missionary who had a significant contribution to the development of Pentecostalism in West Africa, particularly in Nigeria, was S. G. Elton who came as a missionary to Nigeria in 1937. He had contacts with the late Joseph Ayodele Babalola (the pioneer of the 1930 revival in Ilesa, Nigeria) and tried his best to help young Joseph establish God's vision for the Church. He became a mentor to many young Christians who are ministers today such as the late Archbishop Benson Idahosa (1959-1998) of Church of God Missions International, Bishop David Oyedepo of Living Faith Ministries (Winner's Chapel) and Bishop Francis Wale Oke of Sword of the Spirit Ministries.[13] It was Elton who later invited American Pentecostal Tele-evangelists such as the late Gordon Lindsay, the late Oral Roberts, Morris Cerullo, and T. L. Osborne to organise Gospel Campaign meetings in Nigeria. These Evangelists also visited other parts of Africa. Elton was a major player in developing

---

11   The Church of Pentecost was called Gold Coast Apostolic Church until 1962 when it changed to the present name. Since the 1980s, Church of Pentecost has been sending missionaries back to Britain and they have developed a strong partnership with Elim Pentecostal Church. See Chapter Three.
12   Idris Vaughan, Nigeria: *The Origins of Apostolic Church Pentecostalism (1931-1952)*, Ipswich, UK, Ipswich Book Company, 1991, pp. 59-60.
13   Elton played a major role in mentoring and discipling many young people who are today major Pentecostal and Evangelical ministers in Nigeria.

Campus Christianity by introducing Pentecostal teachings into Evangelical Fellowships. It was also Elton who introduced Idahosa to the Church planting concept which later redefined the Charismatic Movement in Nigeria.[14]

Idahosa organised a Gospel Campaign in Ghana in 1977, the same year that Morris Cerullo visited the country.[15] He had a successful Gospel Campaign, but the most significant contribution was the scholarship scheme which saw around 1,000 Ghanaian pastors training at the All Nations for Christ Bible Institute founded by Idahosa.[16] Among those who trained at Idahosa's Bible College were Bishop Nicholas Duncan-Williams of Christ Action Faith Ministries (1979), which is the first Charismatic Church in Ghana and Bishop Charles Agyem-Asare of World Miracle Bible Church (1987), one of the largest Charismatic Churches in Ghana.[17] The Ghanaian Charismatic Movement had its roots in the Christ Apostolic Church of Peter Anim, the Gold Coast Apostolic Church (now Church of Pentecost) of James Mckeom and the efforts of Assemblies of God missionaries. However, Enoch Agbozo's Ghana Evangelical Society (GES) founded in 1973 and the efforts of Scripture Union Travelling Secretaries contributed significantly to Neo-Pentecostalism in the country. It was through this Para-Church organisation and the Scripture Union meetings that many of today's leading Ghanaian Pentecostal ministers were trained.

Interdenominational Evangelical Fellowships such as the Student Christian Movement (SCM), Christian Union (SU), Inter-Varsity Fellowship of Evangelical Unions (IVF) and Christian Union (CU) were introduced into Secondary Schools, Colleges, Polytechnics and Universities across Africa.

---

14   Matthew A. Ojo, *The End-Time Army*, Trenton, NJ, African World Press, Inc, 2006, p. 62.
15   J. Kwabena Asamoah-Gyadu, *African Charismatics*, Leiden, Netherlands, Brill, 2005, p. 111.
16   Kent and Ruth Hodge, *Dispatched to Africa*, Pymble, Australia, Kent and Ruth Hodge Ministries, pp. 86-87.
17   Bishop Charles Agyem-Asare went to the Bible College in 1986.

Scripture Union which particularly focuses on Secondary School students started in Africa around the 1890s. Their activities include speaking at School assemblies, organising Camp and holiday meetings and producing and distributing Christian resources such as the Daily and Power Guides in Schools. As their name implies, Scripture Union's vision is to help young people connect with God's Word. They did achieve this in Africa as many youths embraced this concept of studying the Scriptures and this sowed the seeds for the Charismatic revival which engulf West Africa around 1960-70s. It was this Charismatic or Scripture Union revival (as it is called in Nigeria) which gave birth to Neo-Pentecostalism in West and East Africa. The majority of the Scripture Union Travelling Secretaries partnered with many African students in spreading the Gospel. The transparent character of many of these Travelling Secretaries went a long way to foster friendships that remain even today. A good example can be seen in the ministry of Bill Roberts, Scripture Union Travelling Secretary in Eastern Nigeria in the 1960s. Bill went to Nigeria in 1964 and remained to serve even during a major Civil War in Nigeria (the Biafra War 1967-70). Bill worked alongside an indigene John Onuora and others at the Scripture Union House in Umuahia, present Imo State.[18] Roberts served for five years in Nigeria and fifteen years in Sierra Leone under Scripture Union. While Roberts was serving during the Civil War in Eastern Nigeria a revival broke out which eventually led to the start of Neo-Pentecostal Churches in Eastern Nigeria. Roberts was a mentor to many youths, some of whom have become significant ministers in Nigeria today. Rt Rev. Raphael Okafor, an Anglican Bishop in Eastern Nigeria, was one of the people who Roberts discipled. Roberts' ministry in Sierra Leone was also very fruitful as he was able to train Christian workers who are now holding key positions in the Evangelical community in Africa. Roberts partnered with and discipled men such as David Musa, the first full time Travelling Secretary of Sierra Leone Fellowship of Evangelical Students (SLEFES), Musa

---

18   An interview with Bill Roberts on 5 January 2010 at his Residence in Exeter.

Jambawai, former associate Travelling Secretary of SLEFES, Douglas Carew, former Vice Chancellor of Nairobi Evangelical Graduate School of Theology (NEGST) and presently Old Testament lecturer at NEGST and Aiah Foday-Khabenje, former General Secretary of Evangelical Fellowship of Sierra Leone (EFSL) and currently General Secretary of Association of Evangelicals in Africa (AEA). [19]

In concluding this section, it must be mention that there are independent Pentecostal ministries working as missionaries in Africa. Reinhard Bonnke's Christ for All Nations (CFAN) is an example of this independent ministry. Bonnke organised his first Gospel Campaign in Lesotho in 1967 and since then his team has witnessed some of the largest gatherings in the Continent of Africa. CFAN works in partnership with African ministers, missionaries and Government agencies in spreading the Gospel in Africa. Another independent Pentecostal ministry operating in Africa is Christ Faith Ministries founded by Dr. Kent Hodge. Dr. Hodge first went to Africa to work with the late Archbishop Benson Idahosa in Benin City, Nigeria, in around 1986. Dr Hodge worked with Idahosa for approximately twenty years as the Principal of All Nations for Christ Bible Institute (Idahosa's Bible College) before he went on to found an independent Bible College, Christ Faith Ministries in Jos, Plateau State.[20]

---

19   Bill Roberts is now retired from the role of Scripture Union Travelling Secretary, but he now works with Evangelical Fellowship of Sierra Leone (EFSL). He is involved in training leaders for the Churches in Sierra Leone.
20   An Interview with Dr Kent Hodge at his residence in Essex, England on 4 January 2009.

Chapter Three
Africans in the Dark Continent of Europe

Historical Overview of Africans in Europe

It is often assumed that the presence of Africans in Europe originated from the Trans-Atlantic Slave Trade. This assumption is often pressed to the extreme of thinking that the slave trade is the beginning of black history. This assumption has recently been challenged by black historians as they have managed to trace black presence in Europe back two thousand years. Archaeological and documentary evidence suggests that black people were involved in Roman Britain as slaves and as military men. Around AD 193-211 five hundred North African soldiers were stationed at the Roman military garrison on Hadrian's walls in Cumbria. Little is known about black people in Britain between the third and fourteenth centuries. It has even been argued by Jos Williams that it was the invasion of the Anglo-Saxons which led to the decline of black people in Britain during the fifth and sixth centuries[21]. Whether this has been substantiated or not, it is however clear that from around the fifteenth century onwards European contact with Africans through trade and commerce resulted in an increased number of Africans coming to Britain. For example, it is recorded that a trumpeter of King Henry VIII, John Blanke, was a black man.[22] In 1555 John Locke introduced five

---

21   Mark Sturge, *Look What the Lord had done*, England, Scripture Union, 2005, p. 62.

22   Michael N Jagessar and Anthony G Reddie (eds), *Black Theology in Britain: A Reader*, London, Equinox Publishing Ltd, 2007, p. 31.

Chapter Three Africans in the Dark Continent of Europe

black slaves to England as a result of his slave dealings with Africa. These five slaves were instructed in English and sent back to the Guinea coast (known today as Guinea Bissau) as translators to further England's commercial interests. In 1565 the baptism of a black man called John the Blackamoor was recorded. It is difficult to estimate the number of black people living in Britain around this period, but there was certainly a presence in London given the fact that a German merchant tried to gain a royal license to transport black people to Spain and Portugal in exchange for English captives held there.[23]

As mentioned in the first chapter, the Portuguese explorers began the slave trading using Africans around the fifteenth century. However, by the end of the seventeenth century England dominated the Trans-Atlantic slave trade. This is also known as the 'Triangular Trade' which saw the voyage of Africans to the New Worlds (America and the West Indies). This added to the African Diaspora in Britain. This period of darkness in African history produced some astounding African Christians in Britain. The slave trade was abolished in 1807, and slavery in the British colonies in 1833 and 1838; this also had a dramatic effect on the number of African Diaspora in Europe. The following is a brief description of African Christians who lived in Britain, or visited for some reason from the period of the slave trade till the modern era.

Scipio Africanus (c 1739?): We have fragmented surviving evidence of this man, but the little knowledge we have has identified him with the Evangelical Movement of John Wesley and George Whitefield.

James Albert Ukawasaw Gronniosaw (c 1730-?): He was born in what is known today as Northern Nigeria. He was taken as a slave to the West Indies and then later to North America. He was converted by reading Richard Baxters' book, 'A Call to the Unconverted'. He later became a seaman and a soldier. James met George Whitefield and wrote a book entitled, 'A

---

23   David Killingary and Joel Edwards, *Black Voices*, England, Inter-Varsity Press, 2007, p. 20.

Narrative of the Most Remarkable Particulars in the Life of James Albert Ukawasaw Gronniosaw, An African Prince', as related by him.

Ignatius Sancho (1729-1780): Ignatius Sancho was born on a slave ship by African parents and went to Grenada before he was brought to England as a servant. He was baptised as a Catholic but lived as a committed Anglican. He was a friend of Olaudah Equiano and criticised Christian involvement in the slave trade as opposing what the Gospel teaches. He wrote letters which were published after his death; 'The Letters of Late Ignatius Sancho, An African'.

Philip Quaque (1741-1816): Philip Quaque was from the then Gold Coast (today known as Ghana). He came to England to study as a missionary with the intention that he would return to minister in West Africa. He was ordained as an Anglican priest and married an English woman. He spent ten years in England then returned home in 1766 as a missionary to his people.

Olaudah Equiano (1745-97): He is probably the best known educated African from around this period. Olaudah Equiano was from Nigeria, stolen as a child and sold as a slave first in Africa and later to America. He bought his freedom and later came to England. Equiano later became an author, journalist and an abolitionist. He worked alongside people such as William Wilberforce and Granville Sharp to eradicate slavery. He was also appointed as a Commissary in charge of stores to cater for Africans who were being resettled back in Sierra Leone in West Africa. He married an English woman and his autobiography is a classic, 'The Interesting Narrative of the Life of Olaudah Equiano, or Gustavus Vassa, the African'.

Quobna Ottobah Cugoano (c 1757-179?): Ottobah Cugoano was born in Fante in Gold Coast (Ghana). As a young boy he was kidnapped and sold as a slave to Europeans. He was taken to the West Indies and worked in Grenada before coming to England. He was baptised in 1773 with the name John Stuart.

Ottobah was a friend with Olaudah Equiano and spoke out against the Slave Trade and slavery, writing a book about its evils; 'Thoughts and Sentiments on the Evil of Slavery'.

Phillis Wheatley (1753-1784): She was born in West Africa and taken as a slave to Boston. Phillis, like so many African Christians, believed that it was God's providential plan that brought her to America from Africa. She learned to read and write and became a very good poet; in fact some of her poems were printed in the Boston Newsbook. When George Whitefield died Phillis wrote a poem which attracted the attention of people in Britain. After she was freed as a slave in 1773 she started to speak out against slavery.

Samuel Barber (1785-1828): Samuel was the son of Francis Barber (a friend of Olaudah Equiano and Ignatius Sancho) and his mother was an English woman. Samuel was converted in a Methodist meeting around 1805/06. He became a Sunday School teacher and was very much interested in Evangelism. He later became a Methodist minister and joined the primitive Methodist Movement (known as Ranters). This group of Methodists allowed women to become evangelists.

John Jea (1773-18?): John was born in Calabar Nigeria. At the age of two he was kidnapped and sold as a slave onboard a ship to America. By the age of fifteen he had taught himself how to write and had already become a Christian. He later gained his freedom and became a preacher and seaman. He was a Methodist and travelled to England and Ireland, marrying an Irish woman. John was also a political activist speaking against injustice. He wrote his life story in 'The Life, History and Unparalleled Sufferings of John Jea, The African Preacher'.

John Frederic Naimbanna (?-1793): John Naimbanna was born as a prince in Sierra Leone. He was acquainted with both the white and black settlers who established Freetown as a slave Colony. His Father, who was an African chief, sent John and his brother to Europe to be educated. John came to

London where he was known as 'The Black Prince'. John was an Evangelical Christian and an abolitionist and knew the members of the Clapham Sect. He challenged Eurocentrism, reasoning that Europeans are not superior to Africans.

James Emman Kwegyir Aggrey (1875-1927): Aggrey was born in Ghana. In 1898 he went to study at Livingstone College in the United States. He was later ordained in the African Methodist Episcopal Zion Church and remained in the States as a pastor. Aggrey was an educationist and made several visits to Britain to give lectures.

Gregory Mpiwa Ngcobo (1876-1931): Ngcobo was born in Zululand in South Africa. He was baptised and confirmed in an Anglican mission in South Africa. In 1891 at age fourteen he was sent to England to study. He studied at Sussex and then later at St Augustine's College in Canterbury where he undertook a missionary training course. He worked for the Society for the Propagation of the Gospel and was later ordained as a priest.

Solomon Plaatje (1876-1932): He was born in the Orange Free State in South Africa. He was an active Christian and founding member of the South African Native National Congress (SANNC). He was fluent in many African and European languages. Solomon came to Britain in 1914 with SANNC delegation to protest in parliament about the recent Act legislating the dominance of whites in South Africa. He also used this opportunity to speak on public platforms about the social injustices against Africans. Solomon published a book on the Land Act and came back to England in 1919 to further protest about the racial segregation in South Africa.

It must be mentioned that there were also educated Christian black men and women from the West Indies and America who lived and contributed to the British society during this period. These include men and women such as Joseph Jackson Fuller, Peter Stanford, Celestine Edwards, Harold Moody, Edward Barrett, Henry Beckford, Moses Roper, Thomas L Johnson,

Zilpha Elaw, William and Ellen Craft, Amanda Smith and Mary Prince. I have not given much detail to the history of Caribbean Christians in Britain as that is not the purpose of this book.

The black population in Britain c. 1750 has been estimated at around 10,000 in London and 5,000 outside London.[24] The presence of the majority of these was not significant as many were slaves, seamen, servants and cooks. Only a few rose to become preachers and occupy significant posts in society. The majority of black people during these periods were men, with women constituting a minority. Women were often employed as domestic servants but poverty drove some to prostitution. However this was not the general condition of black women as some had the opportunity to be educated and even become accomplished painters. This was the case of both Dido Belle and Jane Harry who were successful painters during this period (1750).

The abolition of the slave trade did not end the racial discrimination towards black people. While it prevented to some extent dehumanisation of black people, it was however replaced by institutional racism. This is one of the reasons why towards the end of the nineteenth century the majority of black people were still living on the margins of society. Many of them lived in the major ports of London, Liverpool and Bristol due to their occupation (sailors) and because these had been slave ports during the slave trade.

Another factor that led more immigrants to come from Africa to Europe after the abolition of the slave trade was the partitioning and colonisation of Africa. This had its origins in the Berlin-Congo conference of 1884/5. The First and Second World Wars (1914-1945) also saw an influx of African immigrants. This was because soldiers were recruited from African countries to fight in European wars. After the war some of these soldiers decided to stay in Europe, the majority of whom married British women and settled down in England.

---
24   Killingray and Edwards, p. 21.

The efforts of the above African Christians were all within the structures of mainstream Churches such as the Church of England, Baptist, Methodist and Catholic Church. The first African-led Church and mission agency founded in Europe by an African was the African Churches Mission founded in 1931 in Liverpool. It was founded by Daniels Ekarte (c 1890s -1964) who was born in Calabar Nigeria. As a boy Ekarte was influenced by the Scottish missionary Mary Slessor (1848-1915) who worked amongst the Calabar people in Nigeria. Mary influenced Ekarte as a result of her adapting to the African culture. This inculturation helped Mary to stop the killing of twins in Calabar. Ekarte became a seaman and came to Liverpool around 1915. He became a Christian in 1922 and married Lily, an English lady, and they had a son named George. Lily eventually died in 1927 and George was fostered by a neighbour. Ekarte began the African Churches Mission (ACM) in Toxteth, Liverpool in 1931.

Liverpool's prosperity in the mid-nineteenth century depended largely on slave economy. As mentioned above the black population increased during and after the First World War in places such as Liverpool, Bristol and London. One of the impacts of the war on Liverpool was the increase in unemployment and poor living conditions. This was coupled with racial discrimination. For example, the inter-marriages between black men and white women were a major tension in Liverpool; the product of such marriages were 'half-caste' children (today called 'mixed race' or of recent 'dual heritage'), which were rejected by many people in society. This was the socio-economic milieu into which ACM was born.

Ekarte began to organise services in the slums, private rooms and open-air fields for the ethnic minorities of Liverpool. Through local funding he acquired a permanent place to meet. Ekarte's Church became a community centre for both black and white people in the community. He also visited people in prisons, hospitals and in their homes. He became a voice for the poor and marginalised in the society by defending them in his sermons, letter correspondence and public speaking.

Ekarte believed and fought for racial equality. This brought him in direct opposition with the local government and it had negative effects on the ACM. The end of the Second World War brought about the birth of many illegitimate 'half-caste' children resulting from the union between African soldiers and English women. Ekarte decided to transform the ACM into an orphanage for these children and a rehabilitation centre for the women involved. However this hub for the hurting community was later ordered to close and the children transferred to the city's children home. Ekarte was barred from any further contact with the children. The local authorities did this because they could not tolerate an African who was campaigning for racial equality. In addition, financial constraints and the public denunciation of the local authorities by Ekarte worsened the case. After this event the life of the Mission continued but it struggled to survive. Finally in 1964 the local authorities demolished the building housing the Mission. The blow of the Mission shutting down was too much for Ekarte and not long after, in 1964, he died. Ekarte was and remained a hero in the sight of Africans for the great things he achieved in Liverpool.[25]

The 1940 and 1950s witnessed the influx of Caribbean people into England. Several factors led to these immigrants starting their own Churches. One major reason was the fact that many Caribbeans belonged to these Churches back home in the islands, therefore when they realised that these Churches were not operating in Britain they founded them. Another reason was the racial exclusion and abuse experienced from the historic Churches, although it must be mentioned that this was not the universal experience of Caribbeans, as some were welcomed into mainstream Churches. This is one of the reasons why there is still a huge presence of Caribbeans in the historic denominations and today we have Caribbean ministers who are Catholic, Methodist, Baptist and Anglican. Nevertheless, the 1940s and 50s witnessed the formation of

---

25   Marika Sherwood, *Pastor Daniels Ekarte and the African Churches mission*, London, the Savannah Press, 1994, p. 111.

Caribbean Churches in the UK, Churches such as Calvary Church of God in Christ (1948), Church of God in Christ (1952), Church of God of Prophecy (1953), New Testament Church of God (1953), Church of our Lord Jesus Christ of the Apostolic Faith (1957), Wesleyan Holiness Church (1958) and Church of the First Born (1958). Some Caribbean Church denominations originated in the UK such as Bethel United Church of Jesus Christ (1955).[26]

The first waves of African-led Churches in England after the ACM were Church plants of black Americans of African descent. The obvious racial discrimination witnessed by African Diaspora of the late eighteenth and early nineteenth century in America gave birth to a number of African-American denominations such as the African Methodist Episcopal Church, the African Methodist Episcopal Zion Church, the National Baptist Convention of America and the Presbyterian Church of USA. Two of these Churches were planted in England, the first being the African Methodist Episcopal Church in 1966 and the second the African Methodist Episcopal Zion Church in 1970.

The 1960 and 70s witnessed the formation of African Pentecostal Churches in England. This was as a direct result of the independence of African nations in the 1960s from their European colonial masters. This independence gave opportunity for Africans to visit European countries; therefore many Africans came here as students to further their education, work and establish businesses. Diplomats were also deployed to newly establish African embassies and consulates. As they settled down into their new context many became involved in Church plants of their home Churches and others started new ones.

The first phase of Churches planted by Africans was from the African Instituted Churches (AIC). The first of such to be planted in Europe was the Church of the Lord (Aladura)

---

26   J.D. Aldred, *Respect*, Werrington, Peterborough, Epworth Publishers, 2005, p. 96.

planted in 1964 by the late Apostle Adejobi in South London. This Church has its headquarters (HQ hereafter) in Nigeria. Others soon followed such as the Cherubim and Seraphim Church in 1965 (HQ in Nigeria), the Celestial Church of Christ in 1967 (HQ also in Nigeria), Aladura International Church founded by Rev. Father Olu Abiola in 1970. Father Abiola has also established Churches in France, Italy and Germany. Others include Christ Apostolic Church (CAC) Mount Bethel founded by Apostle Ayo Omideyi in 1974 (HQ in Lagos Nigeria), and Christ Apostolic Church (CAC) of Great Britain in 1976 (HQ in Ibadan Nigeria). The first of the Ghanaian Churches to arrive in England was the Musama Disco Christo Church (MDCC) in 1980 which is now being pastored by Rev. Dr Jerisdan H Jehu-Appiah. It must be mentioned here that most of the African-led Churches in Europe are from West Africa, especially from Nigeria and Ghana, however there are other African-led Churches in Europe. For example, the influx of Egyptians, Ethiopians and Somalians has led to the establishment of the Coptic Orthodox Churches in Europe, North America and Australia.

The 1980s and 1990s witnessed a different form of African Pentecostal Churches and it is the phenomenal growth of these Churches that has puzzled missiologists, Church historians and the wider public. Their origins were of humble beginnings, starting as house Churches, community centre Churches, School Churches and small office-space Churches. Some of these Churches have grown to become Church denominations with HQs in Europe from where they conduct missions to other parts of the world. Others have been Church plants from HQs back in Africa. Some of these Churches have acquired abandoned cinema buildings, derelict Churches, massive warehouses or offices and Schools as part of their properties. These Churches are referred to as Neo-Pentecostal/Charismatic Churches (NPC hereafter) because the majority of them originated from the Charismatic revival in West Africa in the 1960s/70s. Nigeria and Ghana play a leading role in the establishment of these Churches in Britain.

The following is a profile of some of these NPCs in the UK:

- Gospel Faith Mission International (GOFAMINT) began in Nigeria by Dr R.A. George in 1956. A branch Church was established in Camberwell, London (God's Heritage Camberwell Assembly) in 1983. This Church is their Headquarters in the UK pastored by Joseph Adeyemo with four other branch Churches and a Bible College (Heritage Bible College). They also have a branch Church in Belgium.
- The Deeper Life Christian Ministry (DLCC) was started in Nigeria in 1973 by W.F. Kumuyi. They began in the UK in 1985 and also have Churches in Belgium, the Netherlands and Luxemburg.
- New Covenant Church was started in the UK around 1985/86 by Rev. Dr Paul Jinadu. They have 41 branch Churches in the UK and Rev Obafemi Omisade is the UK National Overseer.
- The Church of Pentecost started in Ghana around 1937. They began in the UK in collaboration with Elim Pentecostal Churches around 1988/89. Today they have 82 branch Churches in the UK in the major cities such as London, Birmingham, Manchester, Liverpool, Nottingham, Sheffield, Leeds and Glasgow. The present National Secretary is Apostle M.S. Appiah. The Church of Pentecost also has Church branches in other European countries such as Germany, Italy, France, Belgium, Luxemburg and the Netherlands.
- The Redeemed Christian Church of God (RCCG) was started in Nigeria in 1952 by Josiah Akindayomi. They began in the UK in 1988/89 and are the fastest growing Church denomination there. They have more than 375 Churches in the UK and have Churches in Germany, Norway, Spain, Holland, Italy, France, Belgium, Switzerland, Poland, Austria, Denmark, Sweden, Finland, Greece, Portugal, Luxemburg and the Czech Republic. The current General Overseer is

Pastor Enoch Adeboye and the UK National Overseer is Pastor Agu Irukwe of Jesus House in North London. Jesus House is one of the largest black Churches in the UK with a membership of 2,500.[27] RCCG London also organises a Christian Festival called 'Festival of Life' at the Docklands Excel Centre which attracts around 40,000 people every year.[28]

- Bethany Fellowship International of Great Britain was begun in South East London in the 1980s by the present Primate and Vicar of the Church Rev. Dr Prince John Blackson.

- Lighthouse Chapel International Founded by Bishop Dag Heward-Mills around 1988/89 in London. Branch Churches have now been planted in Switzerland, Poland, the Netherlands, Spain, Austria, Germany, Italy, Hungary, Czech Republic, France and Ireland.[29]

- Christ Faith Tabernacle was founded by Apostle Alfred Williams in the UK in 1990.[30]

- Victory Bible International Church was founded in Accra Ghana by Bishop Nii Apiakai Tackie-Yarbio in 1985. The first Victory Church to be planted in the UK was in 1991 by Bishop Clement Asihene. Victory Churches have also been planted in other European countries.

- Kingsway International Christian Centre (KICC) was founded in the UK by Pastor Matthew Ashimolowo in 1992. KICC is the largest Church in Western Europe with a membership of around 12,000 people. KICC has around 21 branches in the UK.

- Praise Valley Temple (PVT) was founded in Accra Ghana

---

27 *Christianity*, August 2006, p. 15.
28 *Keep the Faith*, ISSN 1757-2363, p. 12.
29 Bishop Dag Heward-Mills was mentored by Bishop Duncan-Williams of Christian Action Faith Ministries. He was also involved in a Gospel band in the 1980s with Dr Femi Olowo, now Principal of South London Christian College.
30 From the 28 February-5 March 2010, Christ Faith Tabernacle celebrated its twentieth anniversary.

in 1992 by Bishop Owusu Ansah Bernard. The Church was planted in London and Amsterdam in 1993. Praise Valley Foundation UK (a Para-Church organisation of PVT) was registered as a Charity organisation in 2002.

- Glory House was founded by Rev. Dr Albert Odulele with his brother Vincent Odulele and Dr Jonathan Oloyede in 1993 in the UK.[31] Glory House is one of the largest Churches in the UK with a membership of around 3,000 people.
- Christian Action Faith Ministries was started in Ghana by Bishop Nicholas Duncan-Williams in 1979. The Church arm of the ministries, Action Chapel International (ACI), was established in London in 1993 and pastored then by Paul Adefarasin. The Church is presently pastored by Pastor Dick Essandor.
- New Wine Church was founded by Dr Tayo Adeyemi in 1993 in the UK. New Wine Church in Woolwich is one of the largest Churches in the UK with a membership of around 2,100 people.
- Freedom's Ark Church was founded by Rev. Nims Obunge in 1993 in the UK. Rev. Obunge is also the person behind the Peace Alliance, an initiative to reduce crime in the community. Rev. Obunge is British, of Nigerian parents.
- Christ Gospel Church was founded by Rev. Gabriel Ilori around 1994 in the UK.
- International Central Gospel Church was founded by Dr Mensah Otabil in Ghana in 1984. The first Church plant in the UK was established in 1996 and is currently being pastored by Gracious Selassie-Awoye. The Church has other branches in Italy and the Netherlands.
- House on the Rock was started in Nigeria in 1994 by Pastor Paul Adefarasin. The London branch called the

---

31   Dr Jonathan Oloyede has now left Glory House to start an independent Church; City Chapel in Beckton, London. He is also the Convener of Global Day of Prayer, London.

London Lighthouse began in 1996 and the Church is pastored by Omawumi Michael Efueye.
- Rehoboth Foundation was founded by Rev. Celia Apeagyei-Collins in the UK. Rev. Celia is a mentor to many women leaders in ministry. Her organisation offers mentoring services as well as development and leadership training to men and women.
- El-Shaddai Ministries was started by Dr Ramson Mumba in 1998.
- Centre for World Evangelism was founded by Dr Isaac Danfo in 1999.

The 1990s also witnessed the rise and development of Caribbean independent Pentecostal Churches such as Ruach Ministries led by Bishop John Francis (1994); Rhema Christian Ministries (1996), formerly known as Croydon Rhema Fellowship (1990) led by Pastor Mark Goodridge; Victory Christian Centre formerly led by Pastor Douglas Goodman (jailed for sexual assault); Christian Life City (1996) led by Bishop Wayne Malcolm; Micah Christian Ministries (1998) led by Pastor Denis Wade; The Tabernacle Church (formerly called The Bible Way Church of the Lord Jesus Christ Apostolic) led by Pastor Michael W. White and host of other Churches.

Since the year 2000 there has been an unprecedented increase of NPCs from Africa in the UK. For example, the Everlasting Arm Ministries in Old Kent Road started in the year 2001 and today their membership is around 1,500 people. Winners Chapel founded in Nigeria by Bishop David Oyedepo in 1981 started in Bermondsey London in 2001. The Church is pastored by Pastor David Oyedepo (Bishop Oyedepo's son) and the membership has grown to 3,000 people. They also have Church branches in Manchester and Southern Ireland. Other Churches are Christ Embassy, founded by Chris Oyakhilome in Nigeria around twenty five years ago, which began in the UK in the 2000s. They have 22 Churches in London and 16 Churches outside of London. Word Miracle Church

International founded by Dr Charles Agyin-Asare in 1987 in Ghana. The London Church branch started in Newham, South East London, in around 2005 and is pastored by Rev George Ofei. Finally there is Mountain of Fire and Miracle (MFM) founded in Nigeria in 1989 by Dr Daniel Olukoya. This started in the UK in the 2000s. A trip to Old Kent Road in South East London would reveal the rate of proliferation of African Churches in the UK.

Another feature of African-led Churches in Europe is the Para-Church organisation, or Freelance Mission Agency. These freelance ministries are led by Evangelists from Africa who visits European countries on short-term mission journeys. These Evangelists are more interested in flexible ministries than planting Churches or Church denominations. They establish relationships with a network of Churches or interdenominational ministries in Europe who oversee their evangelistic outreaches. One of the pioneers of this type of ministry to Europe was the late Archbishop Benson Idahosa of the Church of Mission International. Idahosa started the Church of God Mission in 1972 in Benin City, Nigeria. Idahosa began mission outreaches to other countries such as the United States and Ghana in the 1970s. In the 1980s he started visiting the UK and had the opportunity to speak at the National Conference of the Assemblies of God. He also had ministerial opportunities with Elim Pentecostal Churches, especially with Kensington Temple pastored by Colin Dye. He also had a good relationship with Colin Urquhart of Kingdom Faith Ministries. However his greatest alliance in the UK was with Peniel Church in Essex. Idahosa's Church and Peniel formed a partnership and they worked together on mission projects. In an interview conducted with a family who are members of Peniel Church, they mentioned that Idahosa was one of the people who inspired Peniel Church to build a School as a mission tool.[32] Idahosa, before his death in 1998, also visited other European countries such as Switzerland, Belgium, Norway, Netherlands and Russia.[33]

32 An interview with the Cooper family at their residence in Essex on Sunday 14 December 2008.
33 Idahosa has been recorded as visiting around 125 countries of the world

Chapter Three Africans in the Dark Continent of Europe

Other freelance African Evangelists and Teachers who visit the UK are:

- Dr Uma Ukpai of Uma Ukpai Evangelistic Association, Nigeria.
- Dr S.K. Abiara of Agbala Itura (Vineyard of Comfort) Nigeria.
- Prophet T.O. Obadare of World Soul Evangelistic Ministries, Nigeria.
- Bishop Nicholas Duncan-Williams of Christian Action Faith Ministries, Ghana.
- Dr Mensah Otabil of International Central Gospel Church, Ghana.
- Pastor Ransford Obeng of Calvary Charismatic Centre, Ghana.
- Bishop Mike Okonkwo of The Redeemed Evangelical Mission (TREM), Nigeria.
- Ayo Oritsejafor of Word of Life Bible Church, Nigeria.
- Dr Ebenezer Markwei of Living streams Ministries, Ghana.
- Rev. Dr Ampiah Kwofie of Global Revival Ministries, Ghana.
- Bishop Francis Wale Oke of Sword of the Spirit Ministries, Nigeria.
- Rev. Steve Mensah of Charismatic Evangelistic Ministry, Ghana.
- Dr Seth Ablorh of Manna Mission Church, Ghana.
- Dr Tunde Joda of Christ Chapel International Churches, Nigeria.
- Abubakar Bako of Logos Rhema Foundation, Nigeria.
- Dr Samson Ayorinde of World Evangelism Bible Church, Nigeria.[34]

---

before his death. See Benson Idahosa, *Faith for Doing the Impossible*, Benin City, Nigeria, Published by CGM/IWO Publications, 1994, p. 4.

34   This is not an exhaustive list as there are others that have not been mentioned.

A different type of a Para-Church organisation established by an African in the UK is Prayer for Peace in the Congo founded by Rev Jean Bosco Kanyemesha. Different because this Diaspora initiative aims to engage in the political and social-economic situation of Democratic Republic of Congo through advocacy, reconciliation, conflict resolution, poverty relief, provision of services and advancement of human rights. Rev Jean is also the minister and founder of London Fire Church International Fellowship (2002) and through this platform he has been able to raise the standards of ministry among the Francophone and Congolese Churches in Britain.

Since the 1970s there has been a growing presence of African-led Churches in other European countries such as Germany, the Netherlands, Switzerland, Belgium, France, Portugal, Spain, Ukraine and Russia. The first of the African-led Churches established in a European country outside the UK was probably the Celestial Church of Christ founded in Munich Germany in 1974. The Kimbanguist Church, whose members are from Central African countries of Democratic Republic of Congo (formerly Zaire), Congo-Brazzaville and Angola, began with a group of African students in Belgium in 1978.[35] Since then other Kimbanguist Churches have been established in France, the Netherlands, Switzerland, Germany, Spain and Portugal. There was also The True Teachings of Christ's Temple founded and started in Amsterdam, the Netherlands, around 1976/78 by Rev. Daniel Himmans-Arday (the first African-led Church in that country). Other NPCs from Africa have followed since the 1990s, for example the largest Church in Eastern Europe (20,000 people) is the Embassy of God founded by Sunday Adelaja (of Nigeria) in Ukraine in 1994. In Hamburg Germany there is the Christian Church Outreach Mission International (CCOMI) founded by Dr Abraham Bediako in 1991. There is also the Bethel Prayer Ministries International having nine Churches in Germany, seven in Italy, three in France, and two

---

35 Kimbanguism owes its name to Simon Kimbangu (1887-1951) a Belgian-Congolese prophet who founded the Church of Jesus Christ on Earth. Kimbanguism as it is popularly known is one of the largest AICs in central Africa. See Chapter Two.

in Holland, Austria, Switzerland, England and Israel. Other African-led Churches in Germany are the African Christian Church, the Church of the Lord (Aladura) and a French-speaking Congolese Church. Owing to the proliferation of African-led Churches in Europe, the Council of Christian Churches of African Approach in Europe (CCCAAE) was formed in 2001 to establish ecumenical partnerships amongst represented Churches.

African Pentecostal Churches, especially the NPCs, have dominated much of the study on African-led Churches in the Diaspora. However it must be mentioned that there is a concentrated number of Africans in the Historic Churches. There are Africans in the Catholic, Methodist, Baptist, Presbyterian and United Reformed Churches as well as the Church of England and Salvation Army. The majority of Africans in these Churches either belonged to these Churches when in Africa or changed Churches on arrival in the UK. Since the 1970s Africans in the historic Churches have been ordained as clergies and this has resulted in Africans and other ethnic minorities forming caucuses within them. These caucuses exist to cater for the needs of ethnic minorities within the established Churches. In the Church of England the forum is known as the Committee for Minority Ethnic Concern and within the Baptist Union and the United Reformed Church they are known as Racial Justice and Committee for Racial Justice and Multicultural Ministry respectively. The Baptist Union of Great Britain has actually taken a further step in embracing Africans and Caribbeans by formerly apologising for the Trans-Atlantic slave trade.[36] The apology was no mere sentiment because meetings and seminars were organised to follow up the conversation and leaders of the denomination travelled to Jamaica to give the apology in person. Africans in the historic Churches are making their contributions as well as their counter parts in independent Churches. For example, the

---

36   The Baptist Union of Great Britain Council meeting on 14/11/2007, Resolution - An Apology for the Trans-Atlantic Slave Trade printed in *Transform* a Baptist Union of Great Britain's publication, Issue 018, January 2008.

Archbishop of York is an African and he is the first black man to hold the position. Also the current president of the Baptist Union, Rev. Kingsley Appaigyei, is an African and he is the first black man to have held the position. He also pastors one of the largest Churches in the Union, the largest being a Church plant from his Church.[37] Rev. Kingsley's story is of particular interest because of his contributions to the Baptist Union. He came to this country in 1985 to study biblical Hebrew with the intention of going back to Ghana to teach in a seminary. While he was studying for a B.A at Spurgeons' College, he felt called to stay in the UK. His placement Church was Crofton Park Baptist Church where he was well received in 1987-88. After completing his studies, he started Trinity Baptist Church in his house in South Norwood. Trinity Baptist Church under the leadership of Rev. Kingsley has now planted 17 Churches and an orphanage home in Ghana. Two of these Churches are in Italy, one in Denmark, another in the Netherlands and a further Church in Ghana. The Church celebrated the 25 years of ministry of Rev. Kingsley this year in their annual Integrity Conference in April.

The Racial Justice Co-ordinator for the Baptist Union is a black British man of African parents, Rev. Wale Hudson-Roberts. He is also the founder and Chair of African Development Forum (ADF) an organisation that is involved in addressing the issues of poverty in Africa. The London Baptist Association (LBA) Regional Minister for Missions is also an African, Rev. David Shosanya. David is also a co-founder of Street Pastors Initiative, and facilitates the State Black Britain Symposium which offers dialogue between black communities within the UK. African Christians are also involved in established Para-Church organisations such as Christian Aid, Tearfund, Hospital Chaplaincy, School Chaplaincy, Scripture Union, Premier Christian Radio, Christian Concern for our Nation (CCFON) and The Bible Society.

---

37   The largest Church in the Baptist Union is Calvary Charismatic Baptist Church in East London pastored by Rev. Francis Sarpong.

Contributions of African-led Churches in Diaspora

Africans are leading the largest and fastest growing Churches in Europe. This becomes more significant when we consider the fact that the secularisation of European states is causing Christianity to be on the decline. It is because of this decline and coldness towards religion that commentators and African ministers have labelled Europe 'the dark continent'.[38] In addition, Europe is also becoming more anti-religious, especially anti-Christian. The recent cases of the discrimination of a North-Somerset Nurse, a Primary School receptionist and countless others demonstrate that Christianity is no longer favoured.[39]

There are several reasons why Europe has embraced secularism at the expense of religion. The period of the enlightenment ushered in a wave of scepticism and cynicism towards religious hierarchy. This was a result of the paradigm shift popularly known as rationalism; God was deposed from the throne and reason was enthroned. Another reason was Deism which asserted that God created the universe but abandoned it to function on its own. A further factor which dealt a deadly blow to Christianity was Darwinism. The publication of 'The Origin of Species' in 1859 reduced people's confidence in God as a creator. War in Europe, particularly the First and Second World Wars and the Holocaust led people to despair and eventually nihilism. Finally, the sexual attitudes and lifestyles of the 1960s endorsed alternative relationships which led to moral decadence in society. This eventually led to the postmodern shift which asserts that there can be no grand narrative or absolute truth. Several of the respondents were suspicious and wary of labelling Europe the 'dark continent'. This means that not every African minister agrees with the term, their argument being that there are still committed and honest Christians in Europe which is true.

African-led Churches function as social and community

[38] Ogbu U Kalu (eds), *African Christianity: An African Story*, Trenton, NJ, African World Press, 2007, p. 439.
[39] *Daily Mail*, 13 February 2009, p.17

centres for the large number of African immigrants and ethnic minorities in the Diaspora. They serve as hubs for the socio-economic, spiritual and educational needs of Africans in Europe.

These Churches have also provided a space for black people to develop their complex identity and feel included in a country that often excludes them.[40] They have also provided coaching, mentoring and role models for young black people in Britain.

African-led Churches are providers of hope through their inspirational Gospel Music. Gospel singers such as Muyiwa Olarewaju and Riversongz, Dizzy K Falola, Trinity Baptist Church choir, RCCG choir and others have made significant contributions to the Gospel music scene.

African-led Churches also contribute to the renewal and preservation of Christianity in the Western world. Their high regard of Scripture coupled with intense mobilisation for prayers and intercession has helped to preserve a spirituality that thrives in the midst of secularisation. An example of this is the efforts of the Global Day of Prayer which organises strategic prayer meetings for spiritual and social concerns in the UK. Another is the Festival of Life organised by RCCG UK which prays for revival, social ills and the government. African Churches have also preserved Christian heritage in Britain by buying abandoned Church buildings which would have been used by other faith communities.[41]

African-led Churches are contributing to discourses on Global Christianity. The reverse flow in missions from South to North has been a fascinating subject for both religious and secular researchers. The religious researchers include both African and European scholars. Centres such as Birmingham, Oxford, Edinburgh and Bayreuth in Germany are all at the forefront of academic research in the field of African Christianity in the Diaspora.

40   http://www.joealdred.com/?q=node/30.
41   Sturge, M., p. 108.

Africans are also making their contributions in the area of theological and ministerial studies. For example, Dr Femi Olowo founded South London Christian College in 1992. In addition there are African theologians who lecture in Seminaries, Bible Colleges and Universities in Europe. These include Dr Emmanuel Lartey who is one of the early pioneers of Black Theology in Britain at the University of Birmingham, although now lectures in United Sates; Dr Afe Adogame lecturer in World Christianity and Religious Studies at the University of Edinburgh; Allan Anderson Director of the research unit for New Religions and Churches in the School of Historical Studies, University of Birmingham; Rev. Dr George Wauchope tutor for mission education at Queens Foundation for Ecumenical Theological Education (Selly Oak Centre for Mission Studies); Dr Asonzeh Ukah a research fellow in Old and New Churches in the religious Market of South Africa Bayreuth's University, Germany; the late Dr Kwame Bediako who was one of the directors of Oxford Centre for Mission Studies and the late Dr Ogbu Kalu who lectured in the States but was a visiting lecturer to Edinburgh's department of Divinity.

African Christians are also contributing in the area of women's ministries and feminist discourses. Such women include Archbishop Fidelia Onyuku-Opukiri, founder of Born Again Christ Healing Church, who is involved in pioneering women's ministries in an ecumenical approach through Council of Christian Churches of an African Approach in Europe (CCCAAE). Rev. Dr Kate Coleman (the first black woman Baptist minister in the UK) was formerly President of the Baptist Union and is involved in a Para-Church organisation 'Next Leadership' which develops, trains and mentors women as well as men in leadership training. Rev. Celia Apeagyei-Collins, through Rehoboth Foundations, is also involved in the coaching, mentoring and training of leaders.

African-led Churches and ministers are involved with social action issues. Issues such as economic development in Africa are engaged through the agency of the African Development

Forum (ADF), migration issues through migration services provided by Musama Disco Christo Church (MDCC) and other African Churches, gun and knife crime through Peace Alliance (founded by Rev. Nims Obunge MBE) and the Football Academy initiated by Glory House. Jesus House in North London runs various community projects that tackle poverty, injustice and illiteracy programmes in Britain. A recent example of how African-led Churches are involved in social concerns is demonstrated in the Haitian situation. African Pentecostal Churches such as Kingsway International Christian Centre (KICC), New Wine Church in Woolwich, Jesus House and a host of others have responded to the crises in Haiti by donating huge sums of money to relief agencies such as Tearfund and Christian Aid. African-led Churches in other European countries are also engaged with social justice issues. A good example is Sunday Adelaja's Embassy of the Blessed Kingdom of God in Ukraine which is actively involved in the rehabilitation of drug addicts and prostitutes and the feeding of the poor. All the eight African ministers and leaders interviewed for this research are involved in missions and social action.

African-led Churches are contributing to the economic development of Britain through their financial power. The purchase of defunct Church properties, office and School buildings and the use of media all play a significant role in maintaining social infrastructures.

African-led Churches offer objective criticism in regards to the British culture. This is because their culture and worldview is different from Western culture. This critic helps our English brothers and sisters to evaluate their heritage.

They are contributing to unity in diversity in the ecumenical scene through cohesion projects such as the Evangelical Alliance, International Ministerial Council of Great Britain (IMCGB), Council of Afro and Afro-Caribbean Churches (CAACC), Churches Together in Britain and Ireland (CTBI), African Caribbean Evangelical Alliance (ACEA which has now ended due to lack of funds), Global Day of Prayer (GDOP, London), Zebra Project and a host of others. Last year in October an evangelistic and teaching event called Fresh Focus was organised in a joint effort by some African Pentecostal and leading British Evangelical leaders.

The fact that the African-led Churches are certainly contributing to the British society has even been recognised by the Prince of Wales and the Duchess of Cornwall. Prince Charles, in marking his 59th birthday, attended a special thanksgiving service held at Jesus House in recognition of the contribution of Black Majority Churches (BMC) to their communities.[42]

Caribbean Christians in the UK have also made, and are still making, significant contributions. In the writer's opinion they have probably done more than Africans. Caribbean men and women such as those listed below are all contributing positively to the community: the late Phillip Mohabir, founder of African Caribbean Evangelical Alliance (ACEA); Rt. Rev. Wilfred Wood former Bishop of Croydon and the first black Bishop in the Church of England, a true pioneer of Racial Justice in the UK; Rev. Joel Edwards (former Director of Evangelical Alliance) now the current Director of Micah Challenge; Rev. Ermal Kirby chair of the London District of the Methodist Church; Bishop Dr Joe Aldred Secretary Minority Ethnic Affairs for Churches Together in Britain and Ireland and former Director for White and Christian Partnership; Rev. Les Isaac of Ascension Trust through the efforts of Street Pastors; Dr David Muir Public Policy Director for Evangelical Alliance; Noel Robinson, one of the pioneers of British Gospel Music; Rev. Chris Andre-Watson Baptist Missionary Society (BMS) London Area Co-ordinator; Mark Sturge, former General Director of African Caribbean Evangelical Alliance (ACEA), now ended due to lack of funds; Katei Kirby former Chief Executive Officer of ACEA; Dionne Gravesande Head of Churches for Christian Aid; Robert Beckford journalist and theologian; Dr Anthony G Reddie Theologian at Queen's Foundation for Ecumenical

42   http://www.christiantoday.com/article/prince.charles.marks.59th.birthday. with.tribute.to.black.churches/14567.htm.

Theological Education and Ms Pat White moderator of Racial Justice working group of the Baptist Union.

Factors behind the Success of Black Majority Churches (BMCs) Mega Churches in Britain

- Their high view of Clergy breeds strong leadership. The congregation believes in the leadership and they do not enter into debates about issues. The democratic process is not really part of the culture; there are principles of democracy in terms of trustees and leadership, but it is not an open debate.
- The level of faith expectation of its members; the congregation believes in a God who can do the impossible.
- The communal nature of black culture which goes beyond Sunday services.
- Visionary leadership that is ready to take risks and explore new dimensions.
- Holistic approach to mission. Many black Churches give practical help with all aspects of life including business, career, education, finance, marriage and family support. There is no compartmentalising between Church and life; the African worldview is holistic and this plays a factor in incorporating the spiritual and the physical, whilst that of Western culture tends to keep religion out of the public sphere.
- Prosperity Gospel or theology which addresses the socio-economic needs of migrant communities.
- Large number of African and Caribbean immigrants in Britain.
- They act as a social hub for many new immigrants.
- Their dynamic style of worship as expressed through art, dance and graphic design which are very appealing to young people.
- Mission among their own people.

- The financial commitment of the average member is many times ahead of those in well established (centuries old) churches.
- The use of media and ancillary print materials facilitates awareness and attracts people to church services, meetings and activities.
- Marketing and promotion strategies of their Church or ministry through TV media such as Sky.
- Strong prayers and intercessions with fasting.
- African ministers also take spiritual warfare seriously which in the writer's opinion is very much needed in succeeding in ministry.

Criticisms of Black Majority Churches (BMCs)

Black Majority Churches have been criticised since their inception in the 1940s. However the current criticisms have been from both black and white Christians. The following are the major criticisms levelled against black majority Churches:

1. Mission only amongst their own. BMCs tend to attract people of their own nationality such as Nigerians ministering to Nigerians, Ghanaians to Ghanaians, or Caribbeans to Caribbeans. This has been a major concern for many African and Caribbean leaders. All my eight respondents agreed that BMCs outreach is still very much within their caucuses. However, one of my respondents reasoned that racism and exclusion both from the mainstream Churches and society at large is one of the factors for this monoethnic trend. Another reason given by one of my respondents was that Africans or Caribbeans feel more at home in a familiar environment. This is definitely true not only for Africans and Caribbeans, but for all human beings; we all want that sense of belonging and identity in a community. For example, there is also in the UK the Indian Church, Tamil Church, Greek Church, Korean Church and White Majority Churches. The existence of these Churches

demonstrates the fact that this is not only a problem within the BMCs, but one of the general problems of the Church in Britain. Monoethnic Churches have their place and function within the British society, however they must be ready and willing to be multicultural because that is the context in which they serve.

2. Lack of wider involvement and engagement in social action projects. This has been another area of critique against BMCs. Three quarters of the ministers/leaders interviewed agreed that BMCs are not engaging enough with wider social justice concerns such as global poverty and climate change. They were of the opinion that whereas they are involved in local social concerns such as gun and knife crime, immigration issues and socio-economic needs of migrant communities, they are still to mature to engage in global issues. Dr Joe Aldred, Secretary of Minority Ethnic Affairs for Churches Together in Britain and Ireland, said regarding whether BMCs are engaging with social-economic concerns "it is clear that the issue is not one of the absence of social involvement, but, about the depth and breadth of that involvement".[43] One respondent mentioned that BMCs need to broaden their theological worldviews in order to accommodate global concerns such as climate change and global poverty. A few BMC leaders are already engaged with global issues, for example Rev. Joel Edward through Micah Challenge is already tackling global poverty, but what is needed is wider participation of BMC leaders.

3. Prosperity Theology. The preaching of the Prosperity Gospel has been severely criticised and condemned by both black and white Christian leaders. It has been criticised as an import from the United States which cannot work in the UK context. It has also been viewed as a means for Church leaders to exploit the poor. The latter point is valid in some instances, but there is the need for people to

---

43   http://www.joealdred.com/?q=node/30.

understand why this gospel is preached in the majority of the black Pentecostal Churches in the UK. Firstly, Prosperity Theology in the UK must be understood as a contextual theology responding to the economic needs of migrant communities. It must be viewed as an aspect of Liberation Theology which seeks to address the experience of the poor and the oppressed; in this case black people in Britain. When an African immigrant comes into this country the poverty, economic recession and political instability that are the factors of his/her journey automatically dominate, therefore their existence in the UK becomes a matter of survival. This is why coming to the UK for many Africans is like entering the Promised Land. There are a lot of Africans for whom their plane tickets and visa fees (the latter being non-refundable) were borrowed from friends and families. To make matters worse they often have many dependents waiting for them back home in Africa and this is why sending money through Western Union is very important to Africans. These complex financial needs are some of the factors that drive the quest for economic breakthrough among Africans in Europe. Secondly, Prosperity Theology is a means of funding independent BMCs. The Historic Churches often do not have struggle with funding due to several factors: they have been around for longer periods of time than the independent BMCs, they rely on generous legacies and donations of long standing members and philanthropists and they have acquired Church buildings over time which means that mortgages have often been paid. The independent Churches on the other hand are young Churches who rely on the committed giving of their members in order to survive. Having said this, it must be mention that the abusive use of the prosperity message that enriches the Pastor at the expense of the congregation, or its use as a 'magical formula' for success is not Scriptural.

4. Lack of effectiveness of BMCs mega Churches.[44] A quarter

---

44   By mega Churches I mean Churches with an average attendance of 1, 000 congregants or more.

of the ministers/leaders interviewed expressed the fact that being a mega Church does not necessarily mean that it is a successful Church; this is rightly so. There is the need for BMC mega Churches to develop and sustain house groups to disciple their members. Some of these Churches are already doing this, but we are yet to see more of this happening. It must also be mentioned that mega Churches are not just a feature of BMCs; there are mega Churches which are White Majority such as Hillsong Church (5,000), All Souls Langham Place (Anglican, 2,000), Holy Trinity Brompton (Anglican, 1,700) and Soul Survivor outreach festivals which number around 15,000 in attendance.

5. Child abuse and witchcraft. BMCs have been accused of child abuse and witchcraft hunting. The Victoria Climbie enquiries have given BMCs a negative image in the press. It is misleading to label the Churches involved in Victoria's case as 'black-led Churches'. The three Churches identified as culprits include a Church with Brazillian origins, a traditional denomination with a well respected child protection policy and the minister of the third Church was trained in a White-led Church denomination. The main reason why BMCs have been accused of child abuse is because they have not made it very clear what they believe and what they teach. This has not helped the public to have a clear understanding of who these Churches are. On the other hand, irresponsible journalism which has not got all the facts right has given these Churches bad names.[45]

Weaknesses of African-led Churches in the UK

Having looked at the contributions and criticisms of BMCs, in particular African-led Churches, the following are the considered weaknesses of African-led Churches in Britain. These are concerns that need to be addressed for the future existence of these Churches in the UK:

1. Lack of cross-cultural mission strategies.

---

45   http://www.jesus.org.uk/ja/mag_talkingto_oloyede.shtml.

2. Extreme preaching of Prosperity Theology.
3. Lack of unity among African as well as Caribbean Churches. One of the factors for the division among African-led Churches is the fact that majority of African ministers and missionaries came here individually and not corporately as the European missionaries did to Africa. The result is that many African Pentecostal Churches are building their own empires rather than working together. This leads to independency and competiveness among African Pentecostal Churches.
4. Importation of African Christianity without contextualising it in the British culture. In essence; lack of indigenising Christianity amongst the British populace.
5. Lack of theological education that will properly address and shape the ecclesiology and missiology of African-led Churches. It is not that African ministers do not desire to be trained and equipped theologically; to the contrary, the vast majority of the ministers interviewed were theologically trained. The problem seems to be that this has not become a widespread accepted practice among African ministers. The majority of African ministers value the experience that comes from ministering more than the academic study of theology. This is why in the majority of African Pentecostal Churches theology is taught from the pulpit rather than in an academic journal or theological books. In addition, the majority of African ministers are trained professionals such as Doctors, Lawyers, Engineers, Architects and Civil Servants and reason that this previous skill and God's anointing are sufficient for ministry practice.
6. Lack of ecumenical partnership with people of diverse colour and creed.
7. Lack of political engagement.

Chapter Four
Profile of an African Church in Europe: History and Doctrine of Kingsway International Christian Centre (KICC)

Given the large number of African-led Churches in Europe it is becoming difficult for researchers and scholars to keep up with the developments; even a discussion of all the African-led Churches in the UK would be too great a task for one scholar. Therefore the author has selected a major contributor among the African Pentecostal Churches in Europe as a case study in understanding the growth and doctrinal emphasis of African-led Churches. However, a note of caution must be made here; African-led Churches in Europe are not a monolithic movement but are a heterogeneous one, still in the process of change. Therefore the discussion here is an example and would not necessary mean that all African Pentecostal Churches in Europe believe and practice the same set of tenets. It would also be erroneous not to admit and recognise that African-led Churches have certain beliefs and practices in common. This tension between accepting commonalities among African-led Churches and not generalising them needs to be kept in balanced. The terms 'beliefs' and 'practices' have been chosen to explain doctrinal emphasis as suppose to theology. This is because many African Pentecostal Churches are more centred on practical Christian beliefs and their implication for day to day living than philosophical or speculative theology. Kingsway International Christian Centre (KICC) has been chosen as a result of its pioneering work in Western Europe.

History and Growth of KICC

The history of KICC begins with the founder, Matthew Ashimolowo, who was born to an Islamic family on 17 March 1952 in the city of Zaria, Northern Nigeria. When he was four years of age he had chicken pox and was made by his guardian to sleep outside during the night. He was raised in Zaria Kaduna between 1954 and 1964. His Father was a military man and young Matthew was also planning to attend the Nigerian Defence Academy (NDA). After his Secondary School education Matthew found himself a job and alongside this started organising a party for a Social Club to which he belonged and was the Social Secretary. The party he organised was very successful, however later he lost his job and therefore his accommodation. He became a wanderer without a home to live in or any money to look after himself. A friend of his, Matthew Adejumo, decided to accommodate him in Osun State, South-western Nigeria. Matthew Ashimolowo at this stage of his life was very depressed and he turned to drinking heavily. On one particular day, in a drunken state, he came across a Christian tract written by the Evangelical Tract of Canada. After reading this tract he realised that Christianity was very different from Islam; Christianity was more about having a relationship with Jesus whilst Islam was about formal observance of Islamic practices. The tract made an impact on him and he committed his life to the Lord. Some time later one of his Aunties discovered that Matthew had no job and became quite concerned for him. She told him that her Church needed a caretaker and asked whether Matthew was interested in doing the job. Matthew thought, "If this Lady knows the drunk she is trying to ask to come and be their Church caretaker...........And the next day when the Pastor asked me if I had ever drank, I said no no no way I have never drank but of course as at time I was meaning to stop drinking"[46] Matthew accepted the offer and it was while he was working in this Church that his life radically changed.

---

46   *Ovation Magazine*, 2004 (Ovation is a Nigerian Magazine), Fred Akporaye Mgbonyebi, *Stories of Great Men of God*, Nigeria, King's House Publication, 2007, p. 23.

In order to enter the Military School Matthew needed to undertake his A Level studies and it was during this period of his life that he was drawn to the Bible. He studied the Bible with the same passion that he had needed as a Muslim to study the Quran. These Bible studies eventually affected his A Level because the time he was suppose to use to study for his exams, he used in studying the Bible. Not long after this an Evangelist visited their Church and told him, "You look like someone the Lord is calling for his ministry".[47] The Evangelist came back some time later to the Church and enquired about Matthew, giving him the address of the Bible College he had attended. Matthew enrolled in this Bible College in January 1974 and he graduated in 1976. After graduation he was sent to Foursquare Gospel Church in Shomolu, Lagos State where he became the Assistant Pastor of the Church. Within four years he became the Resident Pastor there and had opportunities to speak at Universities and Colleges. He pastored in Nigeria for ten years (1974-1984). Foursquare Gospel Church, Nigeria was receiving many letters from their members who were living in London asking for a Church to be established there. It was decided that a Pastor was needed, therefore Matthew's denomination mentioned to him that they wanted to send him as a missionary to the UK. Matthew had other plans in mind as he was preparing to undertake a Masters Degree in Canada and his visa was already arranged. However Matthew Ashimolowo accepted the call and came to the UK on the 11th of February 1984 as a Foursquare Gospel Church missionary from Nigeria.[48] He began pastoring 11 Adults and 3 Children in London. The congregation grew steadily and increased to 64 people, however later the membership dropped to 16. As a result of this decline he was advised by the co-ordinating ministers to stop pastoring and look for something else to

---

47   Mgbonyebi, p. 23.
48   Foursquare Gospel Church is a North American Classic Pentecostal Church founded in Nigeria in 1955 through the efforts of Harold Curtis in partnership with Nigerians such as the late Dr Samuel Odunaike (former president of Association of Evangelicals in Africa and former General Superintendent of Foursquare Church, Nigeria) and Dr James Abayomi Boyejo (former General Superintendent).

Chapter Four Profile of an African Church in Europe

do. He persevered however and after around eight years of pastoring (1984-1992) the congregation grew to around 600 people.

Matthew Ashimolowo started to perceive that God was calling him to something different from what he was currently doing; therefore he began to seek God through prayers and fasting. He was instructed by the Lord to fast for seventy five days and he obeyed. After fasting he heard the Lord clearly telling him that the river He was about to give was bigger than the one in which he was serving. He handed over Foursquare Gospel Church and started an independent work on 6th of September 1992. Two hundred adults from his previous Church decided to follow him with around 100 children, and that was how KICC began in a rented hall of a North London Boys' School. A year later the congregation had multiplied to 1,000 people and a building at Darnley Road was bought mortgage-free, followed by a Children's Church on the same road twelve months later. By the time the Church was two years old the congregation had doubled to 2,500 people. The Church kept on growing, and in the first six years their number had grown to 7,000 people which caused them to need a bigger property. Miracle Centre (as was later called), a disused warehouse on 57 Waterden Road in the heart of Hackney was bought mortgage-free for £2.7million and was transformed into a 4,000 seat auditorium.[49] The inaugural service was on the 23rd of August 1998 heralding KICC as the largest Church in Britain. The building became a home to four Sunday services, midweek services, Crèche facilities, onsite counselling and extra curricular teachings. They later became the largest Church in Western Europe with around 12,000 people in attendance and 8,000 Church members.

As a result of the 2012 Olympics to be held in London, the UK government requested that KICC relocate from their 9.5 acre plot in Hackney. The Church therefore planned to settle

---

49 The author visited the Church in Hackney in 2003 and 2005. The Auditorium was a magnificent building and would definitely have inspired anyone who appreciates beautiful architectural work.

at Beam Reach Development Park in Rainham, Essex which had been identified by the London Development Agency as a suitable location for their community complex. KICC planned to build a multi-purpose community centre with an 8,000 seat auditorium, a gymnasium, refectory, media suite, Chapel, memorial garden, bookshops, child care facilities and in-house computer training centre. The Church applied for planning permission which the London Thames Gateway Development Corporation rejected, stating that there were objections from Havering Council and the local community.50 KICC has appealed, but in the meantime, the Church has moved from the Miracle Centre in Hackney to the Land of Wonders in Hoe Street in Walthamstow in East London. The Land of Wonders holds six services every Sunday.51

KICC has continued to grow at a phenomenal rate with a network of Sunday morning Chapels and Branches nationally and internationally. For example, they opened their Ghanaian branch in 2002 and have a further branch Church in Lagos, Nigeria. KICC runs a weekly TV and Radio programme called Winning Ways. This programme is an international ministry which is broadcasted through God Channel and Trinity Broadcasting Network (TBN) in Europe, Africa, USA, Asia and the Middle East. In 2007, KICC launched their TV station called KICCTV which is available on Satellite TV (Sky). Winning Ways is a major conference which the Church organises annually both at home and in Africa, particularly in Ghana and Nigeria. Another major annual conference is the International Gathering of Champions (IGOC). Other conferences include Winning Women hosted by Pastor Yemisi Ashimolowo (Pastor Matthew's wife), and Singles Summit. They also hold their Watchnight service which is held annually on New Years' Eve. The Church has a Kingsway Bible Institute which runs baptismal, membership and discipleship classes.

50   *London Evening Standard*, 4 September 2009, p. 2, http://www.thisislondon.co.uk/standard/article-23740235-mega-church-appeal-fails.do.
51   The author visited this Church 6 January 2008 as part of his field research.

In addition they have a training institute which trains men and women for leadership roles, ministry and pastoral work and is open to people from outside the Church. They also run a telephone counselling service called Hopeline; this counselling service covers crises and legal, financial, career, marital and other issues. In addition, the Church has home groups all over the UK called Caring Heart Fellowships. Pastor Ashimolowo is a prolific writer who has written over sixty books. One of his books, 'Tongues of Fire' was the winner of the Nigerian Booksellers Award. Other of his titles include, 'The Coming Wealth Transfer' (2006), 'Be the Best' (2006) and 'What is wrong with Being Black?' (2007).

The vision of KICC is to: **'Grow Up, Grow Big, Grow Together'**:

- ❖ **Grow Up** in knowledge, perspective, conviction, skill and character in God's Word.
- ❖ **Grow Big** by fulfilling the Great Commission, using every medium available (TV, radio, newspaper and other mediums) to evangelise the Word.
- ❖ **Grow Together** in unity and family spirit.[52]

The organisational structure of the Church places the Senior Pastor as the head of the Church. Pastor Yemisi Ashimolowo is the Resident Pastor of the Headquarter Church in Walthamstow. There are various leaders undertaking a variety of responsibilities as ministers, deacons or divisional, departmental or Caring Heart Fellowship leaders. The Church has a Board of Trustees of which Pastor Agu Irukwe of Jesus House is a member. Finally, the Church has a Senior Management Team which runs the day-to-day activities of the Church Office in Bromley by Bow, East London.

The history of KICC and the life of their senior pastor have been subjected to criticism and scrutiny by the UK government. This was evident during the 2002-2004 enquiries by the Charity

[52] KICC *Church Brochure*.

Commission. In March 2002 there was a routine review by the Charity Commission in which they reported, "The Charity (King's Ministries Trust) has in place an impressive portfolio of policies and procedures for both staff and trustees and is striving to standardise procedures and practices across their operational divisions".[53] However in June of the same year the Charity Commission opened a statutory inquiry into KICC. Then on 28th of November 2002 the Commission appeared without warning at the KICC headquarters with two Receivers and Managers to take over management of the Church. The press release stated, 'The watchdog has taken this temporary action in order to protect the Church's assets as part of an ongoing investigation into concerns about its governance'. David Rich, the commissioner's Head of Investigations in London said, 'The aim of the investigation stated that the Head of the Commission's investigation was to work with the Senior Pastor and other trustees to enable the Church to continue on an improved footing...Services and activities are expected to proceed as planned'.[54] The press release undoubtedly brought the integrity and public reputation of the Church and Pastor Matthew Ashimolowo under suspicion. Moreover, this inquiry followed shortly after that of Pastor Douglas Goodman of Victory Christian Centre who was eventually jailed for sexual assault and abuse of power. The implications were very damaging to KICC and Pastor Ashimolowo. The Commission proceeded with their investigation into three particular issues; firstly, to investigate whether money has been inappropriately paid to members of the Trustees, secondly, the quality of governance and thirdly, to ascertain whether the Church's assets were at risk. KICC was vindicated on all three concerns and money was not paid inappropriately to the Church's Trustees or the Senior Pastor. It is legal for a charity to pay their Trustees; the problem had been that KICC was paying its trustees without the correct wording in their ten year old constitution. Therefore the

---

53   *Power without Accountability*: The Charity Commission as Regulator, Association for Charities Report June 2004, p. 51.
54   *Power without Accountability*.

constitution only needed amending. Regarding the quality of governance, a new independent charitable company was created as opposed to a charity trust. This was a legal matter which did not warrant Receivers and Managers in the first place. Finally, there were no assets at risk. This was already stated in the routine check by the Charity Commission in March 2002. The process of the enquiry cost KICC around £1.2 million, cancellation of their Church activities both home and abroad and more importantly their reputation was marred.

Despite these setbacks, Pastor Ashimolowo is still very much loved and respected by his congregation, fellow black ministers and many Black Majority Churches. He has been and remains a role model for many young black men and a positive influence in society. It is ironic to discover that after the investigation the Charity Commission approved an annual salary of £80,000 for Pastor Ashimolowo making him the highest paid Chief Executive Officer of any Charity in the UK as at 2005. What they arguably failed to do was to restore his reputation through the press.

Beliefs of KICC

Belief in God

KICC, like the majority of Western Churches, believes in God. This God is Supreme and is the creator of the Heavens and the Earth. As far as KICC and many African Pentecostal Churches are concerned, evolution is not a viable alternative to God as creator, neither is the 'big bang theory' nor intelligent design without God. It is also not popular among African Pentecostal Churches to be a theistic evolutionist; that God created everything visible and invisible is strongly affirmed in these Churches. This belief is rooted in Scripture (Genesis 1 and 2, Job 38-42 and John 1: 1-14) and many of the Ancient Near Eastern cultures which have many creation myths about the creation of the world.[55] African cosmogony also asserts

---

55   The Ancient Near Eastern cultures of the Old Testament believe that gods and not God created the world. That God and not gods created the world was one of

that God, the Supreme Being, created the world. KICC do not believe in polytheism and pantheism, but they do believe in the Trinity of the Godhead (Father, Son and the Holy Spirit) as the majority of Western Churches do. KICC also believe that God is the provider of all material and spiritual blessings. He is the God of impossibility; in essence they believe that God can do miracles and that God will provide for the needs for his people. This becomes very practical for day-to-day sustenance because whenever in need or trouble, the first thing to do is to trust God and pray.

Belief in Christ

Like many Western Churches, KICC also believes in Christ and his atoning work on the cross. The virgin birth, death and resurrection of Jesus are taken very seriously. It is not debated whether they actually happened or whether they are just myth language to express concepts; they are believed to have happened in history and they form the basis of what it means to be a Christian. This belief in the literal virgin birth, death and resurrection of Jesus is common among African Pentecostal Churches. The person of Jesus, human and divine, is also held in high esteem. However it seems that many African Pentecostal Churches hold to Christology from above as opposed to Christology from below. This means Christ divinity is emphasised more than His humanity. The miracles of Jesus, especially the records of casting out demons, are considered significant for today. That Jesus suffered and died in substitute for us as sinners and that he resurrected has universal implications. This universalism is not the type that is optimistic about all humanity being saved irrespective of their religion, but rather, it is only through Jesus that humanity can be saved.

Belief in the Holy Spirit and His works

KICC believes in the third person of the Trinity and His renewing work. Baptism of the Holy Spirit is seen as different

---

the distinguishing marks of the Israelites in the Old Testament

from water baptism. To seek to be baptised by the Holy Spirit is an experience that is emphasised among Pentecostal Churches, whether black or white. Another emphasis, which is not common to all African Pentecostal Churches, is the experience of speaking in tongues as a visible sign of the baptism of the Holy Spirit. It is these Churches' belief that the gifts of the Spirit, as enumerated in 1 Corinthians 12 and Romans 12, are for the Church today and are very important for Christian maturity and evangelism. KICC and the majority of African Pentecostal Churches do not believe that the gifts of the Spirit ceased with the Apostolic Age. The fivefold ministry gifts of Ephesians 4: 11-13 are also believed to be operational today. The implication is that there can be Christians called by God into the Apostolic and Prophetic offices today. The Holy Spirit is also understood as a person and not as a wind or force (John 14: 17, 26). Another emphasis by black and white Pentecostal Churches is the day-to-day guidance given by the Holy Spirit. This is usually termed 'being led by the Spirit' or 'being open to the leading of the Spirit'.

Belief in Salvation

As mention above salvation is only through believing in the atoning work and the person of Jesus Christ (Acts 4: 12). The term 'being Born Again' is an expression common to many African Pentecostal Churches. Many West African Pentecostals as well as white Evangelicals believe that Church attendance does not equal salvation. Christian parents also do not guarantee salvation; therefore emphasis is laid on a personal conversion experience. One practical implication of this is that testimony, the telling of ones conversion story, plays an important role in KICC and many African Churches. KICC also believes that being saved now does not guarantee automatic admission to heaven. Christians have choices and we can fall from Grace; in this sense they are more Armenians than Calvinists. 'Once saved forever saved' does not fit into the doctrinal emphasis of the majority of West African Church.

Belief in the Bible

Belief in the Bible plays a crucial role in many Church traditions and denominations. However what makes this belief different in many African Pentecostal Churches is the fact that the application of the Bible is very crucial, rather than the exegesis of it. KICC as well as the majority of African Pentecostal Churches have a high view of Scripture. This means that the science and art of Biblical criticism with all their various departments are not considered important in the preaching and teaching of the Bible. For example, listening to Pastor Yemisi Ashimolowo preach from the text Isaiah 43: 18-19, she dwelt more on the application of what these verses meant for the people today rather than discussing whether it was written by Proto Isaiah, Deutero Isaiah or Trito Isaiah.[56] Numerous black and white Evangelical Christians are often perplexed by this approach to preaching and teaching, but it seems that many African Pentecostal Churches are not engaging with exegesis because African worldview is parallel to the worldview of the Bible. In addition, many Africans can easily identify with Bible characters in that they are experiencing what those characters went through. To illustrate this, Israelites were exiled into foreign countries in the Old Testament; Africans in Europe are presently in Diaspora. This similar experience also leads many Africans to view themselves as continuing the Bible story. However, the emphasis of application at the expense of understanding the text in its original context is something that African Pentecostal Churches will need to address if they must be more relevant to the culture of the UK. The development of a new hermeneutics is needed if they are to contextualise the Gospel to reach people in Western culture.

KICC and other African Pentecostal Churches view the Bible as authoritative, inspired by God and infallible. This is why it

---

56 The author visited the Church on 6 January 2008. Pastor Yemisi Ashimolowo preached on, "Stepping into Something New". Proto Isaiah, Deutero Isaiah and Trito Isaiah is Biblical critics' multiple authorship of the book of Isaiah. These alternative authorships is used to argue against the traditional view which favours Isaiah as the author.

is believed as God's Word to humanity, first revealed to Israel, then to the New Testament Church, and of relevance to us today. Therefore they do not admire any teaching or preaching that is not grounded in Scripture through Bible quotation or reading. African culture and customs are very much based on oral culture rather than written culture and this plays a large part in African ministers' ability to quote large sections of the Bible. Finally, like many Protestant Churches in the West, African Pentecostal Churches hold the sixty six books of the Protestant Bible as God's Word; therefore Apocrypha and the Gnostic Gospels are certainly not recognised.

Belief in the Church and mission

KICC and many African Pentecostal Churches believe that it is only those who are 'Born Again' who are part of the Church. Members of these Churches are therefore those that have confessed Christ as Lord. Depending on which African Church they attend, some can view Christians from other Churches as nominal Christians or 'just religious people' without the 'real faith'. Some even have the extreme view of thinking that they are the only true Church. KICC networks with Churches in other continents, particularly in North America and Ghana. Their leadership style is closer to Episcopalian than to congregational because ministers are more respected and obeyed. The leadership of the Church commands authority and this reflects African culture where elders and spiritual leaders are honoured and respected. This type of leadership style has been abused in many Pentecostal Churches irrespective of race, but its dynamics are a strong vision and fast decision making process. The majority of African Pentecostal congregations prefer strong visionary leadership, therefore they are happy to follow their Charismatic leaders rather than debate with them. KICC believes in women in leadership and this is evident through the ministries of Pastor Yemisi Ashimolowo and other women in the Church. Some African Pentecostal Churches embrace women leadership, while others see their role as subordinate to male leaders.

Evangelism is certainly crucial to the vision of KICC and this is why it is stated in their vision, 'To share the Good News of Jesus Christ with the 11 million people resident in London.'[57] The Great Commission in Matthew 28: 19-20 is taken very seriously by KICC. Overseas mission is achieved through media technology, Gospel Campaigns and conferences. It is of particular interest that KICC, an African Pentecostal independent Church in Europe, is actively involved in mission enterprise in West Africa. The Winning Ways Gospel Campaign attracts around 30,000 participants in Ghana and Nigeria.

Belief in Prosperity

KICC, as well as the majority of African Pentecostal Churches, believe in God prospering his people financially, materially, in health and in education. They believe that the Gospel has a 'total package' affecting every spheres of life. This is why they believe in emotional and physical healing reasoning that if Jesus Christ went about doing good and healing all oppressed by the Devil then he can do the same today. They believe that God can heal through the blood of Jesus and in the name of Jesus, His word or through prayers. Testimonies of healing abound from their Church publications and oral testimonies in their services. Deliverance from demonic oppression is also another feature of many African Pentecostal Churches. This has become the sole ministry of some of these Churches and has been abused on occasions. However African Christians still believe that demons exist today and that they can harm people, but through strong prayers and fasting demons can bow to the power of Jesus. KICC no doubt preaches and teaches financial prosperity; this is evident in their TV programmes, Pastor Ashimolowo's books, special services to raise money for projects and the giving attitude of its members. Tithes and offering are very important and play a key role in developing the Church and maintaining its huge yearly budgets. If there

---

57   KICC Headquarter Church website, http://www.kicc.org.uk/Church/Vision/tabid/45/Default.aspx

is any area that the Church has received criticism, it is in their emphasis of prosperity message.

Practices of KICC

Water Baptism

Water Baptism is a major practice of KICC and this is usually undertaken by an individual after foundational Bible teachings through Kingsway Bible Institute. The mode of Baptism is immersion in the water in the name of the Triune God. Adult baptism is favoured as opposed to infant baptism. Adult Baptism is also a common practice among African Pentecostal Churches and many Western Churches.

Marriage and Home Life

KICC and many African and Western Evangelical Churches view marriage as an institution ordained by God (Genesis 2: 20-25). This belief implies the seriousness and sanctity in which engagement and marriage should be approached and conducted. This is why sex and pregnancy before marriage are not encouraged. In addition, alternatives such as polygamy, bigamy, co-habitation and civil partnerships are frowned upon. KICC organises seminar which addresses issues facing single men and women such as 'what to do while waiting for the right person, purpose in life and how to make a good decision when choosing a spouse.

Giving

As mentioned above tithes and offerings play a major role in the development and maintenance of KICC and various African Pentecostal Churches. The reason why KICC has been able to buy millions of pounds worth of property mortgage-free is because of how serious and committed their Church members are in giving to the Church. Members also give in expectation of God's blessings. The practice and emphasis on giving is common to African Pentecostal Churches.

Daily Devotion

KICC, as well as many African Pentecostal Churches, encourages its members to engage in a daily personal study of the Bible. In addition, personal worship and private prayers are also practices that KICC encourages its members to do regularly. This builds mature Christians who daily wait on God to lead and guide them. This also means that the congregation do not rely too much on the Sunday services to be nourished by the minister.

Prayers

KICC and the majority of African Pentecostal Churches believe in the power and efficacy of prayers. Prayer meetings are a major part of the worship of these Churches. These prayer meetings can take the form of watch-night services, vigils, prayer and fasting and special events. A typical African style of praying is someone leading the prayer topics after which the congregation all pray together loudly. Prayers are usually done with the congregation standing and some even like to pace around the room. Room is given for the use of the gifts of the Spirit as well sharing from the Scriptures. Some African Pentecostal Churches are still in the habit of praying for their enemies to die. This is as a result of extreme use and understanding of the Old Testament.

In concluding this section, the beliefs of KICC and the majority of African Pentecostal Churches are considered Evangelical. Their passion for the Bible as God's Word helps them to preserve Christian values and spirituality that survive in the midst of oppression and persecution. However, one weakness of this is the literal interpretation of Biblical text which at times does not do justice to the context. This is one area where sharp distinction can be drawn between European Evangelicals and African Pentecostals. However, the beliefs and practices of some African Christians in Europe are not in total contrast to that of Western Evangelicals; this is probably because they share similar origins located in the European Reformations of the fifteenth century.

Chapter Five
Concluding Observations

The findings of this research work have implications for Church history, missions and ecumenical relations. Throughout the years Church history has often been written from a Western perspective, and while these voices are not bad in themselves this could easily overlook and misunderstand minority voices. This work has attempted to capture recent developments in the history of Christianity in the West, this history being considered from an African perspective. This is because Africans are now making significant contributions to Christianity in the West. One practical implication of this is that Western Bible Colleges, Seminaries and Departments of Religion and Theology will perhaps need to reconsider what is being taught in Church history and mission modules, and also whether their teaching staffs reflects the racial diversity of ministers in Europe today.

The study has implication for missions considering the fact that missions are no longer a Eurocentric initiative but Africa, Asia and Latin America are all playing their part. European Christians must be willing to learn from African Christians, and vice versa, if missions are to be accomplished in Europe. One practical suggestion is for our European brothers and sisters to seek to understand more about their own culture through listening to the critique that their African brothers and sisters have to offer regarding what they have observed. An outsider's perspective on culture is needed in order to realise and discern what would normally be taken for granted or overlooked.

The third implication is for ecumenism. As Evangelical Christians the Great Commission is a priority that must be taken seriously, and one in which African as well as European Christians has a part to play in Europe. We cannot afford to build our separate empires both reasoning that we will win Europe for Jesus. African Christians as well as Western Christians must make a conscious effort to bridge the gap that separates us. Dr Jonathan Oloyede at a Global Day of Prayer leader's reception admonishes leaders from various Church traditions that it is time for White Majority Churches and Black Majority Churches to work together.[58] This is already happening and this is evident in the partnership that exists between Jesus House pastored by Agu Irukwe and Holy Trinity Brompton presided over by Nicky Gumbel. For this type of ecumenical partnership to happen frequently, we must remember and reconsider the prayers of our Lord in John 17. We must also reflect and act on Paul's theology of Jews and Gentiles now forming one body united under Christ.

African-led Churches in the Diaspora have travelled a long journey from racial discrimination and exclusion to emerge as many of the fastest and largest growing Churches in the West. They have made significant contributions to global and local Christianity and have particularly developed as refuge centres for African immigrants and other ethnic minorities' whose needs have not been met elsewhere. However African Churches still have a long way to go in breaking down racial barriers in order to reach out to the wider British indigenes and Europeans in general. For this to happen, African-led Churches will need to develop new approaches in the areas of cross-cultural communication and Biblical Hermeneutics and to embrace ecumenism.

---

[58]   Global Day of Prayer London, Leaders Reception on 11 February 2010 at West Ham Football Club.

Glossary

African Churches were Churches that seceded from Mission Churches in Africa towards the end of the Nineteenth century. Despite their separation their organisational structure, leadership style, doctrinal position and Church tradition remain essentially European.

African Church Movement is a generic term used to classify the African and Ethiopian Churches. In addition, it is also used to define the Church elite in nineteenth century Africa who were campaigning for the independence of African states.

African Instituted Churches (AICs) are Churches that were initiated by Africans for Africans in Africa from around the Nineteenth century onwards. They are also called African Independent Churches or African Initiated Churches. These Churches have different names in various parts of Africa. In Nigeria some are called *Aladura* Churches (*Aladura* meaning praying people). In Ghana some are called *Sumsum sore* (Spirit Churches). In East Africa some are termed *Roho* Churches (Churches of the Spirit) and *Arathi* that is prophetic Churches. In South Africa they are called Zion or Apostolic Churches.

African-led Churches are Churches led by Africans in Europe, with Africans constituting the majority or part of the congregation. These include African-led Churches in the Historic Churches, African Instituted Churches in Europe and African Neo-Pentecostal Churches in Europe.

African Pentecostal Churches includes some African Instituted Churches (AICs) and African Neo-Pentecostal

Churches (NPCs). These are Churches that lay emphasis on the baptism of the Holy Spirit with the evidence of speaking in tongues, Gifts of Spirit, Healing, deliverance, miracles and vibrant worship.

Black Majority Churches are Caribbean, African and (of recent) South American Churches in Britain.

Charismatic Churches as used in this work are Churches and Para-Church ministries which were formed out of the Charismatic Movement in Africa around 1960/70s. The term is also used to describe Churches which were formed out of the Charismatic renewal of North America and Britain in the 1960s.

Charismatic Movement refers to the revival which started in West and East Africa in Schools, Colleges, Polytechnics and Universities through the agency of Interdenominational Evangelical Fellowships, indigenous charismatics and charismatic missionaries and ministers. The term is also used to describe the renewal which engulfed mainstream Churches in North America and Britain in the 1960s.

Classic Pentecostals refers to the first Pentecostal Churches inspired either by the Welsh revival of 1904 or the Azusa Street revival of 1906. These Churches include The Apostolic Church Britain, Elim Pentecostal Churches, Apostolic Faith Mission, Assemblies of God and Foursquare Gospel Church.

Ethiopianism is the term used to express African nationalism. This is because Ethiopia, apart from Egypt, was the first kingdom to express and revolt against imperialism and white supremacy.

Ethiopian Churches are African Churches in South Africa which seceded from Historic Churches and drew their inspiration from Ethiopia's political and religious independence from European influence.

Evangelical Christians are a major section of the Protestant

Churches. Their origins are traced back to the Evangelical Revival of John Wesley in the eighteenth century in England. The American version of this revival is termed the Great Awakening led by George Whitefield, a contemporary of John Wesley. Evangelical Christians are very passionate about spreading the Good News and they love to abide by the Scriptures.

Historic Churches as used in this book are Western Churches such as Roman Catholic, Anglican, Baptist, Presbyterian, Reformed and Congregational.

Mainstream Churches as used in this book are Historic Churches with the addition of Quakers and The Salvation Army.

Mission Churches are Churches founded by European missionaries in Africa from the period of the nineteenth century.

Neo-Pentecostal Churches (NPCs) are independent Pentecostal Churches in Africa of which majority were born out of the Charismatic revival of the 1960s and 70s in West Africa. The term is also used to describe other Pentecostal Churches that are not Classic Pentecostal Churches.

Pentecostalism as a modern Church Movement started around 1900 in Topeka Kansas in the United States through the teachings and Bible College of Charles Parnham. The 1906 revival that occurred in Azusa Street in Los Angeles through the ministry of William Seymour also laid the roots of Pentecostalism as a Church Movement. Pentecostalism is now a global phenomenon recognised in all the continents of the world; however, its growth has been significant in Africa, Asia and South America. Pentecostals are best defined by the Baptism of the Holy Spirit with the emphasis of speaking in tongues. In addition, this Church movement is characterised by emphasis on gifts and move of the Spirit, healing, revival meetings, miracles, prophetic giftings and free and ecstatic worship.

Bibliography

Adogame, Afe, Gerloff, Roswith, Hock, Klaus (eds), *Christianity in Africa and the African Diaspora*, London, Continuum International Publishing Group, 2008.

Aldred, Joel, *Respect*, Werrington, Peterborough, Epworth Publishers, 2005.

Anderson, Allan, *African Reformation*, Trenton, NJ, African World Press, 2001.

Anderson, Allan and Hollenweger, Walter (eds), *Pentecostals after a Century*, Sheffield, Sheffield Academic Press, 1999.

Asamoah-Gyadu, Kwabena, *African Charismatics*, Leiden, Netherlands, Brill, 2005.

Ashimolowo, Matthew, *Be the Best*, London, Mattyson Media, 2006.

Ashimolowo, Matthew, *What is wrong with Being Black*, Shippensburg, PA, USA, Destiny Image Publishers, Inc, 2007.

Ayegboyin, Deji and Ishola, Ademola, *African Indigenous Churches*, Lagos, Nigeria, 1997.

Bonnke, Reinhard, *Living a Life of Fire*, Orlando, Florida, E-R Productions LLC, 2009.

Chike, Chigor, *African Christianity in Britain*, Milton Keynes, Author House, 2007.

Cugoano, Quobna Ottobah, *Thoughts and Sentiments on Evil of Slavery*, London, Penguin Books, 1999.

Equiano, Olaudah, *The Life of Olaudah Equiano, or Gustavus Vassa, the African*, Mineola, NY, Dover Publications Inc, 1999.

Bibliography

Eusebius, *The History of the Church*, Middlesex, England, Penguin Books, 1965.

Fatokun, Samson, *History and Doctrine of the Early Church*, Ibadan, Nigeria, Enicrwonfit Publishers, 1999.

Garlock, Ruthanne, *Fire in His Bones*, Tulsa, Oklahoma, 1981.

Gronniosaw, James Albert Ukawsaw, *A Narrative of the Most Remarkable Particulars in the Life of James Albert Ukawsaw Gronniosaw, An African Prince, as related by Himself*, Great Britain, Hard Press, nd.

Hanks, Geoffrey, *70 Great Christians*, Kaduna, Nigeria, Evangel Publications, 1992.

Jagessar, Michael and Reddie, Anthony, *Black Theology in Britain*, London, Equinox Publishing Ltd, 2007.

Kalu, Ogbu (eds), *African Christianity An African Story*, Trenton, NJ, African World Press, 2007.

Kalu, Ogbu, *African Pentecostalism*, Oxford, Oxford University Press, 2008.

Kenny, O.P., Joseph, *Early Islam*, Nigeria, Dominican Publishing, 1997.

Killingray, David and Edwards, Joel, *Black Voices*, England, Inter-Varsity Press, 2007.

Korieh, Chima, Nwokeji, Ugo (eds), *Religion, History and Politics in Nigeria*, New York, University Press of America, 2005.

Metzger, Bruce, Coogan, Michael (eds), *The Oxford Companion to the Bible*, Oxford, Oxford University Press, 1993.

Mgbonyebi, Fred Akporaye, *Stories of Great Men of God*, Nigeria, King's House Publication, 2007.

Ojo, Matthews, *The End-Time Army: Charismatic Movements in Modern Nigeria*, Trenton, NJ, African World Press, 2006.

Omoyajowo, J.A., *Makers of the Church in Nigeria (1842-1947)*, Lagos, Nigeria, CSS Bookshops Limited, 1995.

Onwubiko, K.B.C., *History of West Africa (AD 1000-1800)*, Onitsha, Nigeria, Africana-Fep Publishers Limited, 1985.

Onwubiko, K.C.B., *History of West Africa (1800-Present Day)*, Onitsha, Nigeria, Africana-Fep Publishers Limited, 1985.

Ositelu, G.A., *Expansion of Christianity in West Africa*, Abeokuta, Nigeria, Visual Resources Publishers, 2002.

Ositelu, Rufus Okikiolaolu Olubiyi, *African Instituted Churches*, London, Transaction Publishers, 2002.

Pobee, John and Ositelu, Gabriel, *African Initiatives in Christianity*, Geneva, WCC Publications, 1998.

Sancho, Ignatius, *Letters of the Late Ignatius Sancho, An African*, London, Penguin Books, 1998.

Sanneh, Lamin, *Translating the Message: The Missionary Impact on Culture*, Maryknoll, NY, Orbis Books, 2009.

Sanneh, Lamin, *West African Christianity: The Religious Impact*, London, C. Hurst and Co, 1983.

Sherwood, Marika, *Pastor Daniels Ekarte and the African Churches Mission*, London, the Savannah Press, 1994.

Sturge, Mark, *Look What the Lord has Done: An Exploration of Black Christian Faith in Britain*, England, Scripture Union, 2005.

Sylvester, Nigel, *God's Word in a Young World*, London, Scripture Union, 1984.

Ter Haar, G, *Halfway to Paradise: African Christians in Europe*, Cardiff, Cardiff Academic Press, 1998.

Vaughan, Idris, *Nigeria: The Origins of Apostolic Church Pentecostalism (1931-1952)*, Ipswich, UK, Ipswich Book Company, 1991.

Wagner, Peter and Thompson, Joseph (eds), *Out of Africa*, California, Regal Books, 2004.

Webster, J.B., *The African Churches among the Yoruba 1888-1922*, Oxford, Oxford University Press, 1964.

Other Sources (Magazines, Church Publications, Articles and others)

Christianity, August 2006.

Black Majority Church-What's in a Name? A Discussion Book by Barnardo's CANDL Project.

Daily Mail, 13th February 2009.

Keep the Faith Magazine, Reaching the Heart of the Black Community, ISSN 1757-2363.

Kingsway International Christian Centre (KICC) *Church Brochure*.

London Evening Standard, 4 September 2009.

Ovation Magazine, 2004.

Power without Accountability: The Charity Commission as Regulator, Association for Charities Report June 2004.

Technicolour in Black and White by Jonathan Oloyede.

The Baptist Times, Thursday 6th of August, 2009.

The Embassy of the Blessed Kingdom of God for All Nations *10 years of Grace.*

Transform, Baptist Union of Great Britain's publication, issues 018, January 2008.

Winner's Chapel *Church Brochure,* Bermondsey, London.

Going through the eye of the Storm by Pastor Matthew Ashimolowo, DVD, 25 January 2007.

Internet Sources

http://www.ccel.org/ccel/schaff/anf03.toc.html.

http://www.lausanneworldpulse.com/themedarticles.php/973.

http://www.religiousfreedom.com/Conference/Germany/abiola.htm.

http://www.joealdred.com/?q=node/30.

Reverse in Ministry and Missions: Africans in the Dark Continent of Europe

http://www.jesus.org.uk/ja/mag_talkingto_oloyede.shtml.

http://www.christiantoday.com/article/prince.charles.marks.59th.birthday.with.tribute.to.black.churches/14567.htm.

http://www.thisislondon.co.uk/standard/article-23740235-mega-church-appeal-fails.do.

http://www.kicc.org.uk/Church/Vision/tabid/45/Default.aspx.

About the Author

Israel Oluwole Olofinjana is from South-western Nigeria and lived there for 26 years before relocating to the UK. He is an insider coming from a Pentecostal background and was actively involved in a Pentecostal Church in Ibadan, Nigeria for a period of 9 years. During his undergraduate days at the University of Ibadan he was involved in the Ibadan Varsity Christian Union (IVCU) which is renowned for its Evangelical heritage. Israel is now part of Brockley Churches Together, a local ecumenical initiative in South East London. He is also involved with Global Day of Prayer London (GDOP), a prayer movement that embraces different denominations and racial backgrounds.

He holds a **Certificate in Ministry** from Grace Bible institute, Ibadan, Nigeria, has a **BA (Hons) in Religious Studies** from the University of Ibadan, Nigeria and **MTh** from South London Christian College. His research interests include Church History (African Pentecostal History), Biblical hermeneutics and Christian Apologetics. He has presented papers and published articles on African Churches in Europe. Israel is an Ordained and Accredited Baptist minister and co-pastors Crofton Park Baptist Church, a multicultural Church in South-East London. He is happily married to Lucy Olofinjana.

Lightning Source UK Ltd.
Milton Keynes UK
09 June 2010

155338UK00002B/1/P